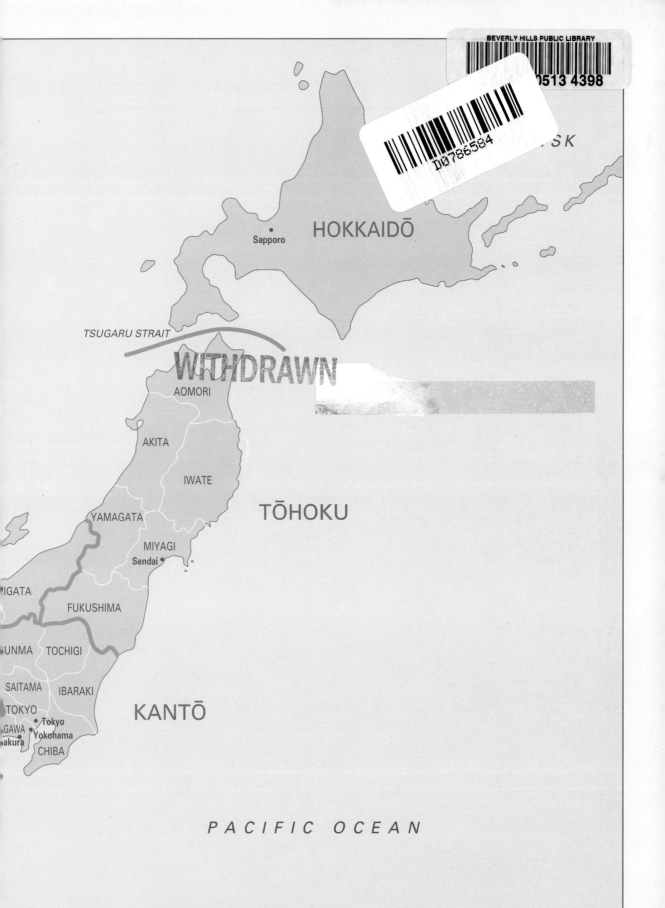

SK

HOKKAIDŌ

Sapporo

TSUGARU STRAIT

AOMORI

AKITA

IWATE

TŌHOKU

YAMAGATA

MIYAGI
Sendai

IGATA

FUKUSHIMA

UNMA   TOCHIGI

SAITAMA   IBARAKI

TOKYO

KANTŌ

GAWA   Tokyo
akura   Yokohama

CHIBA

PACIFIC OCEAN

JAPANESE HOMES AND LIFESTYLES

JAPANESE HOMES AND LIFESTYLES

An Illustrated Journey through History

Kazuya Inaba
and
Shigenobu Nakayama

Translated by John Bester

KODANSHA INTERNATIONAL
Tokyo • New York • London

NOTE: Japanese names appearing in the text before 1868 are given in the Japanese order, with surname preceding given name; names after that date appear with surname following given name.

Distributed in the United States by Kodansha America, Inc., 575 Lexington Avenue, New York N.Y. 10022, and in the United Kingdom and continental Europe by Kodansha Europe Ltd., 95 Aldwych, London WC2B 4JF. Published by Kodansha International Ltd., 17-14 Otowa 1-chome, Bunkyo-ku, Tokyo 112-8652, and Kodansha America, Inc.

Originally published under the title *Nihon-Jin no sumai: jūkyo to seikatsu no rekishi* by Shōkokusha Publishing Co., Ltd.

00 01 02 03 10 9 8 7 6 5 4 3 2 1
ISBN 4-7700-2391-X

CONTENTS

The Modern Period (1868–PRESENT)   93

PREFACE

JAPAN NOWADAYS is increasingly thought of as an *urban* culture—a "nationwide metropolis," as it has sometimes been called. As high-rise construction has run riot, even in relatively smaller, out-of-the-way towns, the former insistence on architecture's primitive, earthbound roots seems to have peaked—the usual scenario in a mature democracy. An extreme instance was the Museum of Modern Art's exhibition entitled "The Un-private House" (New York, 1999), which was an attempt to chart the putative assimilation of domestic landscape into the quasi-public realm. By contrast, regardless of how urbanized and up-to-the-minute Japan has become since World War II, the Japanese house and its lifestyle are still far from expressing such a point of view.

The present book on the Japanese residence by Kazuya Inaba and Shigenobu Nakayama, with its reference to a continuum of "lifestyles," undertakes to explain the evolution of the domestic envelope and the retention, until now, of a Japanese architecture that merges cohesively with its surrounding urban design. There is a sense in which shelter and residence have ever been at the core of all architectural design, inviting, so to speak, a psychology of dwelling. The Japanese residence of the medieval period, whether rural or palatial—and there occurred a cross-fertilization, as the authors explain here—remains, somehow, a badge of Japaneseness, with the *tatami* mat and sliding *fusuma* or *shōji* door/window panels that to many represent a special, virtually unique, way of life and thought.

This work seeks not to mystify, but to objectify and to explain the evolution of the Japanese house—not, until John Bester's distinguished translation, for the outsider but for the ordinary Japanese reader as "insider." Nor is the "*tatami* mind" its goal, since woven straw matting, to take only a single example, is itself a relative latecomer to the Japanese house and its fittings—and likewise to its contextual lifestyle. Instead, the authors present an illustrated capsule history of successive developments from the use of fire in prehistory right down to the advent of Westernization at the time of the Meiji Restoration in the nineteenth century. Finally, the crucial period of reconstructive transformation during the mid-Showa era in Tokyo and lesser urban centers is addressed in the last chapter.

As for *tatami* and the rest, such recognizably traditional features of Japanese lifestyle make their ordered appearance around the middle of this book, in the two chapters entitled "The Medieval Period" and "The Edo Period." Tradition is explained along with the emergence of guilds, the development of new carpenter's tools—the two-man ripsaw and bench plane, ten regional variations of the farmhouse (*minka*), and the important development of the "castle town." This story is, once more correctly, interwoven with the origin and, eventually, the maturation of the *shoin* style. This centers about the palace style of reception room with its raised dais, the ancestor of the surviving Japanese-style room often still a common feature, whether in cheap tract dwellings, restaurants and hotels, public mass-housing (*danchi*), or upscale "*mansion*" blocks of flats or apartments.

As in almost all contemporary societies, a tale of country and city has molded the built environment. Thus, in Japan, as elsewhere, this is the product of a spatio-economic dialectic—not merely of climate and geography, as claimed by most premodern accounts, whose influence has extended well into the present century. Japanese scholars tend to be specialists, with little respect for or appeal to the general reader. Those non-Japanese wanting the bigger picture—including students of architecture and design needing a general idea of a diversely elaborate and, sometimes, elaborately simplified building culture—will be grateful for the wealth of concise line drawings in this book and their matching technical terms.

Furthermore, those wishing to look in greater interpretive detail at Japanese pictorial art will find useful guidelines to a domestic context represented, frequently in great detail but often without explanation, in screens, scrolls, and wood-block prints. Catalogues of traditional Japanese household items or glossaries of tradesmen's terms of the past are widely available, whereas for the specialist in English, who has no Japanese, the principal such handbook as regards the context of built form is Nishi and Hozumi's *What is Japanese Architecture?* (Kodansha International, 1983), supplemented possibly by the relevant volumes in Kodansha International's Japanese Arts Library, notably *Early Buddhist Architecture in Japan* (1980), *Architecture in the Shoin Style* (1984), and *Japanese Castles* (1986).

More recently, as regards the tools of the traditional craftsman, see William H. Coaldrake, *The Way of the Carpenter* (Weatherhill, 1990), which effectively supplements Heino Engel's more generic *Measure and Construction of the Japanese House* (Tuttle, 1990) and Kiyoshi Seike's *The Art of Japanese Joinery* (Weatherhill, 1977).

The story of Japanese residential architecture is brought up to date here, with reference to one or two well-known Modernist houses, and one of the famous Case Study dwellings of the 50s. However, the messiness of the present-day metropolis (what has been called its concentration on *content*, as opposed to form) is of necessity left to the imagination. My own The *Making of a Modern Japanese Architecture: 1868 to the Present* (Kodansha International, 1987) attempts to make sense of the architecture of the entire modern period since Meiji, and, notably as regards the present story, those residences by the architect Kazuo Shinohara that, since the 60s, have appeared coldly machine-like but are at the same time conceived abstractly as works of art in usually urban, and therefore increasingly chaotic, surroundings. There can scarcely be a final word on a *status quo* that is anything but fixed. Nevertheless, it is of interest to listen to what the indefatigable, and internationally known, Japanese house designer Tadao Ando has to contribute to this debate, in Katsuyoshi Matsuba's *Ando Architect* (Kodansha International, 1998).

In any case, whether the work of Shinohara or Ando, or other younger men and women, the best and most arresting contemporary residences in Japan will be viewed with manifestly greater appreciation and understanding if they are looked at from the perspective of the present volume.

David B. Stewart

The Prehistoric Period

Paleolithic Age
(BEFORE 10,000 B.C.)

Jōmon Period
(CA. 10,000 B.C.–CA. 400 B.C.)

Yayoi Period
(CA. 400 B.C.–CA. 300 A.D.)

Burial Mound Period
(CA. 300–CA. 590)

Japan is an archipelago made up of approximately four thousand islands, stretching from Hokkaidō in the north to Okinawa in the south. A cold current flows down from the seas north of the archipelago, while a warm current moves up from the south, the two mingling in the Sea of Japan and the Pacific Ocean with marked effects on the climate and natural features of the land. One effect is that the inhabitants of its northern areas are obliged to lead a semi-snowbound existence for about half the year, while those of the southernmost islands enjoy a more or less perpetual summer. It follows that the homes of the Japanese show a close connection with such natural features.

It was not until about ten thousand years before the birth of Christ that Japan became an archipelago and acquired its present climate and physical features. Until then, it was joined by land to the continent and partially covered for much of the time by glaciers. It was in this period that it was inhabited by the Naumann

elephants and mammoths whose remains have been unearthed in recent years.

Geologically speaking, the glacial age belongs to the Pleistocene epoch, and remains of human dwellings have been found in the particular stratum that represents it. The sites of these dwellings were usually caves or overhanging rocks. Even they, however, had to meet certain conditions. There had to be the right amount of sunlight, warmth, and humidity, as well as sufficient space and ventilation. Guaranteeing a place to live amidst a hostile environment, caves provided human beings with their first "homes."

During the glacial period, there were spells when the glaciers receded. The climate was mild, the number of deer, wild boar, and other animals suitable for hunting increased, and broadleafed evergreen forests spread, so that men left their caves and began to travel in search of animals and plants to serve as food. It is conceivable that Paleolithic people from the continent crossed over into what is now Japan, but so far

■ Cave Dwelling

no definite conclusion is possible. Even so, it is becoming apparent that human beings lived in various parts of Japan as early as 10,000 B.C. The connection between them and the Pale-olithic men of the continent will almost certainly become clearer in time.

It was in the Jōmon period that the ancestors of the Japanese first began to leave clear traces of their ways of life. They settled in pit dwellings, made earthenware pottery, and used tools other than stone implements, living by hunting, fishing, and gathering. Unlike in the glacial period, the climate was mild, the islands surrounded by sea and blessed with many hills and rivers, so that the early inhabitants had access to an abundance of small animals, fish, shellfish, and other foods. In particular, western Japan—areas to the west of the Kantō plain—was thickly covered with broad-leafed evergreen forests providing good supplies of a variety of acorns as well as rhizomes such as kudzu and bracken. The gathering of such vegetable foods led in time to the beginnings of primitive agri-culture, including the cultivation of various potatoes and other root crops, foxtail millet, barnyard grass, and other grains for which the slash-and-burn technique was employed.

In the Yayoi period, the techniques of culti-vating rice in paddies were introduced to Japan from China by way of Korea. Rice quickly became the cornerstone of Japanese agriculture, largely owing to the foundations provided by the prim-itive slash-and-burn methods of the Jōmon period. Rice cultivation brought major changes not only in diet but in daily life as a whole. People began to gather in villages so that they could cultivate the rice paddies through organized, communal efforts. A number of such villages would eventually unite to form a larger village, and so on until small "states" (kuni) began to be formed in various parts of the country. By the Burial Mound period (ca. 300–ca. 590; but per-sisting in some areas to a much later date), the agricultural economy had developed to the point where it was possible to bury the leaders who ruled the states in huge tumuli. Buildings, too, began to include not only the pervasive pit dwelling but also raised storehouses and raised dwellings, so that the home ceased to be simply a shelter for sleeping in and began to convey associations of power and wealth.

■ Paleolithic Campsite

The First Pit Dwellings

In the Paleolithic Age, when people abandoned life in caves and went farther afield in search of plants and animals for food, they were obliged to fashion new dwellings with their own hands. In doing this, they sought to re-create conditions similar to those in a cave. They dug away at the surface soil till they reached the diluvial layer, where they could take advantage of the earth's natural warmth. At this level it was possible to obtain a fairly constant temperature and degree of humidity, and the interior would remain relatively uninfluenced by the climate above ground. The same stratum, consisting

largely of hard clay, allowed rainwater that had seeped into the pit to run off.

Digging a pit also had the advantage that the earth produced in the process could be heaped up around it to form an artificial embankment. By creating this embankment, the inhabitants acquired close to twice the amount of vertical protective space that they would have had otherwise.

In a way of life that depended chiefly on hunting, gathering, and fishing, it was enough if a dwelling provided a shelter from the depredations of nature and wild animals. The outside space was considered part of the dwelling, providing a place to cook and eat, to live in during the day, and to interrelate with other human beings. The

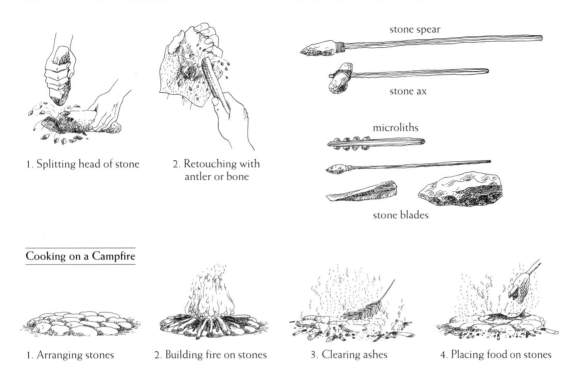

Making a Chipped Stone Tool

1. Splitting head of stone

2. Retouching with antler or bone

Types of Chipped Stone Tools

stone spear

stone ax

microliths

stone blades

Cooking on a Campfire

1. Arranging stones

2. Building fire on stones

3. Clearing ashes

4. Placing food on stones

dwelling itself was simply a place to sleep.

This form of dwelling, known as a pit dwelling, was formerly believed to have been confined to cold, northerly areas, but in recent years the remains of similar types of dwellings have been found in warm, southerly climates. It seems safe to assume that the pit dwelling was in use all over the globe in the latter part of the Paleolithic Age.

The Use of Tools and Fire

The invention of tools was a major step forward for human beings, enabling them to make far more effective use of their hands.

The first material chosen was stone, which was both readily available and harder than bone, which made it useful in hunting. In the first stage, such tools were made by splitting a rock to produce pieces that could be used as a spearhead or club for killing animals. Later, implements were made by chipping off flakes of

stone with bone or horn to be used as knives and spearheads. Around the end of the Paleolithic Age, microliths composed of flakes of stone were attached to a piece of wood, thus creating something like a saw.

It is not known for certain when human beings first started using fire, but it seems likely that once they had begun to live in caves, they procured embers from naturally occurring fires, making use of them for heating and cooking. They probably also used fire for warding off beasts of prey.

Once people had begun to roam far away from their caves, the transportation of such sources of fire became crucial. This problem was solved by inventing a portable source for producing fire in the form of flint. Since pit dwellings were barely large enough to sleep in, with no room for a fire at all, people began to make outdoor stone fireplaces, cooking directly over the flames or making use of heated stones.

Hunting, Gathering, and Agriculture in the Jōmon Period

It was around ten thousand years ago that the Ice Age came to an end and the climate first approximated its present state. Around that time, Japan took the form of an archipelago, no longer connected by land to the continent. The surface of the sea rose, forming deep inlets all around the coast, with a corresponding increase in the availability of fish, shellfish, and other maritime sources of food. On the other hand, the melting glaciers formed rivers that carried silt downstream, creating deposits that provided a home for a wide range of flora and fauna.

For a time, human beings carried on the habits of the Ice Age, shifting their dwellings from place to place while hunting, fishing, and gathering, but eventually they began to seek out places suitable for permanent settlement.

With the increase in supplies of food, they acquired techniques of firing clay to make cooking utensils, thus inaugurating the history of pottery. In making these vessels, they impressed patterns on the exterior using rope or a spatula. Such vessels are known as Jōmon ("rope pattern") pottery, and the age characterized by such pottery in Japan is known as the Jōmon period, distinguishing it from the Paleolithic (pre-pottery) Age. These earthenware vessels were used not merely to hold food and the like, but for cooking as well. By increasing the ways that organic substances could be prepared for eating, pottery made some previously inedible substances available for consumption, thus in effect increasing the food supply.

In addition to the spear, the bow and arrow also came into use for hunting. Dogs were domesticated and employed in capturing prey as well as for defensive purposes. Pitfalls were used to capture larger animals.

Along with animal meat, abundant supplies of fish and shellfish (eaten either boiled or dried) were an important source of food. People worked in groups, not only to catch salmon and

slash-and-burn field

shell mound

■ Jōmon Settlement

trout as they swam upstream, but also to hunt whale and dolphin from dugout boats. With the realization that hunting in large numbers was a good way to increase the amount of food, kinship groups began to establish permanent settlements. The sites chosen for such settlements were usually on the ridges of hills, where it was easy to descend into valleys for water and to move from place to place along the ridges.

The open area at the center of the settlement served as a burial ground. It was apparently believed that the dead would be reborn, and a wake was held in a structure dedicated to that

shell
mound

burial ground

campfire

pitfall

purpose. The burial took place after several days of feasting. The grave was set off by a marker, and offerings were placed before it. The surviving circles of stone and pebble-floored and raised-floor structures apparently served as the final abodes of the dead.

By sometime around the middle of the Jōmon period, in the Kantō and other areas to the south where broad-leafed evergreen woods flourished, nuts such as chestnuts and acorns, miscellaneous grains such as buckwheat, beans, and barnyard grass, and root vegetables such as taro and yam were becoming important food-stuffs. In addition to gathering them in their natural state, people began to cultivate them on slopes near their settlements. Noticing that vegetation seemed to flourish in the wake of a forest or brush fire, they began deliberately to set fire to woodlands to create new fields, or to burn the stubble left after a harvest and use the ash as fertilizer. Such slash-and-burn methods made it possible to secure vegetable sources of food in a planned manner, supplementing what was gotten by hunting and fishing. Thus daily life gradually became more stable, and the population increased rapidly.

drying place

■ Pit Dwelling Interior

The Jōmon Pit Dwelling

The pit dwelling, originally a form of shelter devised during the glacial period, was continued into the Jōmon period even after the development of permanent settlements. As such settlements were formed and food became relatively easy to obtain, more space became necessary, so that the family could not simply sleep in their shelter but could also use it as the center of family life.

The fireplace, which until then had been located outside, now began to be installed indoors, where it heated the living space. Cooking pots could be conveniently arranged around it. A shelf was suspended over the hearth so that fish and meat could be dried and preserved; it also served to

disperse the warm air, spreading heat throughout the room.

The fireplace in the Jōmon period was usually situated in the center of the pit dwelling: first, because the distance to the ridgepole was greatest at that point and thus the danger of the roof catching fire the least, and, second, because it facilitated eating and sleeping around the fire for the family.

The surrounding embankment served to keep out the wind and rain and also fulfilled a structural role by supporting the base of the slanting timbers that formed the principal material of the roof. Consequently, it was important that the embankment be solidly packed in order to ensure the dwelling's durability.

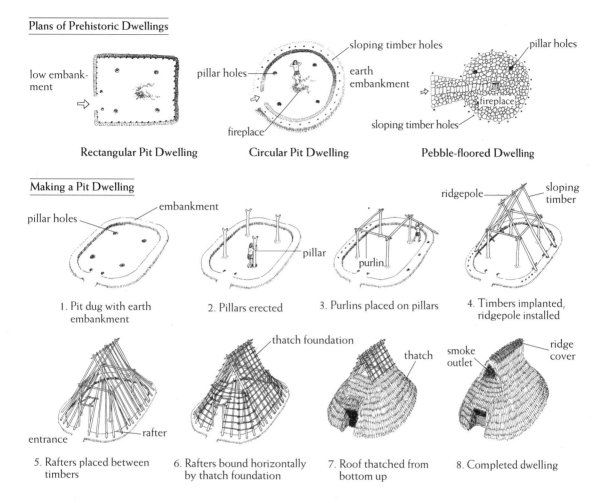

low embankment

pillar holes

sloping timber holes

earth embankment

fireplace

pillar holes

sloping timber holes

fireplace

Rectangular Pit Dwelling　　**Circular Pit Dwelling**　　**Pebble-floored Dwelling**

Making a Pit Dwelling

pillar holes

embankment

pillar

purlin

ridgepole

sloping timber

1. Pit dug with earth embankment

2. Pillars erected

3. Purlins placed on pillars

4. Timbers implanted, ridgepole installed

thatch foundation

thatch

smoke outlet

ridge cover

entrance　　rafter

5. Rafters placed between timbers

6. Rafters bound horizontally by thatch foundation

7. Roof thatched from bottom up

8. Completed dwelling

Changes in the Jōmon Pit Dwelling

In the early stages of the Jōmon period, the pit dwelling was square or rectangular in plan, but toward the middle of the period it took on a circular shape.

In the initial stage, when there was no fireplace within the dwelling, the pit was shallow. There were no pillars within the pit, but rather roughly hewn branches or slender tree trunks were implanted around the periphery and drawn together at the top to form a roof.

Toward the middle of the Jōmon period, with the switch to a circular plan, from four to eight pillars were erected in a square or circle within the interior. The fireplace was centrally located. At the same time, the pit itself became deeper, and the bank surrounding the dwelling corre-spondingly higher. The structure of the roof consisted mainly of sloping pieces of wood stuck into the surrounding bank, the pillars inside acting as props to prevent the sloping timbers from bending or breaking. The roof was thatched with rushes, reeds, or other grasses, the thatch reaching down close to the ground.

Toward the end of the Jōmon period, these pit dwellings were sometimes built on a very large scale, with several fireplaces within the same structure, but in and around the Kantō area an unusual type of house, the "pebble-floored" dwelling, was built. No pit was dug in this case, and the floor was covered with a layer of round pebbles. Often a stone pillar was erected at the rear of the fireplace, so it seems possible that such structures were used in connection with wakes, festivals, or prayer to the gods.

Rice Cultivation in the Yayoi Period

Agriculture of the slash-and-burn type, for the cultivation of vegetables and miscellaneous grains, had existed from around the middle of the Jōmon period, but toward the end of that period a new type of agriculture arose in the northern Kyūshū area. This new type, the cultivation of rice in paddy fields, spread all the way from western Japan to the Hokuriku and Kantō regions within a few centuries.

This period associated with rice cultivation is known as the Yayoi period. It lasted from around the third century B.C. to around the third century A.D.

The short-grain rice that was brought to Japan is of a different strain from the long-grain rice grown in China to the south of the Yangtse river, but resembles that grown in the areas north of the Yangtse and in southern Korea. Therefore, it is believed that the short-grain rice more suitable to cultivation in cool areas came to Japan from somewhere along the lower reaches of the Yangtse, via the south of Korea, to northern Kyūshū in Japan. It seems probable that the same people who brought the rice also brought agricultural implements, methods of storing and cooking rice, and other customs and manners from their home countries.

This rice culture spread rapidly, thanks to the basis provided by the already existing Jōmon-period slash-and-burn culture. However, if yields were to be increased, large amounts of labor would be required to carry out irrigation and water-control projects. As a result, it became necessary for people to work together—not just in small, blood-related settlements but in larger settlements depending on territorial ties. In this way, the village (*mura*) was born.

First situated near the foothills, villages were eventually located on open, level ground, where it would be easy to draw water for the paddies. To oversee the large numbers of people who lived in these villages, leaders were necessary. These leaders must not only possess a good command

moat

raised storehouse

■ Yayoi Village

of agricultural techniques but had to be well acquainted with the changes of the seasons and maintain their authority by praying to the gods of nature at seasonal festivals and transmitting the wishes of the gods to their people.

While rice cultivation made it possible to preserve foodstuffs in a planned fashion, it had the disadvantage of creating differences of wealth and giving rise to conflict between villages.

Arriving from Korea along with the culture of rice cultivation, iron implements found use as agricultural tools, while bronze ware, in the

well

dōtaku

storage pit

square moated tomb

form of swords, spears, *dōtaku* (bell-shaped cere-monial objects), and the like, were used in ritu-als and at festivals. The appearance of these two types of metal objects was to spur the develop-ment of the previously existing stone and wooden implements and promote agricultural productivity.

Although the village was originally a commu-nity created to support the new rice culture, as production steadily rose this community came increasingly to be seen as a clan that worshiped the same ancestral gods. Around each village a defensive moat was constructed, and a rice

storehouse provided a focal point around which were grouped some ten or so pit dwellings. One can imagine that when a festival to celebrate a particularly good harvest was held in the open space around the storehouse, the sound of the *dōtaku* bell being struck served as a means of spiritually uniting the community. When the vil-lage leader died, he or she was not buried in the village graveyard, but was interred reverentially in a moated tomb.

gable

boarding

"rat repeller"

"rat repeller"

pillars embed-
ded in earth

■ Raised Storehouse

The Raised Storehouse—
Symbol of the Yayoi Village

The rice-growing culture was accompanied by techniques for constructing buildings to store the rice. From these emerged the raised storehouse (*takakura*).

The method of harvesting rice used in the Yayoi period involved gathering the heads of rice individually with a narrow-bladed stone knife, enabling the harvester to separate the rice from the miscellaneous grains that were mixed in with it. The heads were then put in the storehouse with the husks still on them, since the rice kept better that way. To prevent the rice from being eaten by rats, "rat-repellers" (*nezumikaeshi*) were fastened to the pillars at a point immedi-

ately below the storehouse floor.

The storehouse was usually quite small, only two meters by three meters in size. The roof was gabled, the entrance being on the gable side. The walls, consisting of overlapping boards, were usually not very high, because rice stacked to a great height would not only be poorly ventilated (and thus be in danger of spoiling) but the weight from the rice would damage the floorboarding. Since the gable side served as an entrance and exit, the ridgepole and gable roof were sometimes extended to prevent rain from entering the storehouse.

As the repository of the village's hard-earned annual harvest of rice, the raised storehouse was a symbol of communal life. Historically, it is the origin of the type of Shintō shrine architecture

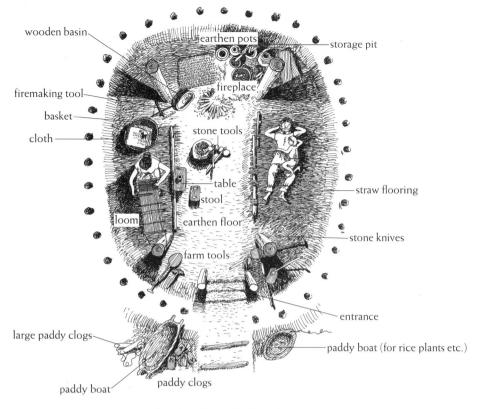

wooden basin
earthen pots
storage pit
firemaking tool
fireplace
basket
stone tools
cloth
straw flooring
table
stool
stone knives
loom
earthen floor
farm tools
entrance
large paddy clogs
paddy boat (for rice plants etc.)
paddy boat
paddy clogs

■ Inside a Yayoi Pit Dwelling

seen at Ise Shrine (dating from the third century) and elsewhere. Even now, shrine compounds often contain a building whose name (*hokora*) originally meant "rice storehouse," apparently harking back to the raised storehouse.

The Interior of the Yayoi Pit Dwelling

Even after the advent of the raised-floor store-house in the Yayoi period, the pit dwelling remained the main form of human habitation. In plan it resembled the pit dwelling of the Jōmon period, but the way the interior was organized had changed greatly.

The major new features were the shifting of the fireplace from the center of the room to the side opposite the entrance; the digging of a storage pit near the fireplace for pottery, grain, and so on; and the establishment of a place for preparing food.

It also seems possible that the area close to the entrance, being near the only source of light, was used for repairing or storing agricultural implements.

The central earthen-floored space, bordered by pillars, appears to have been used for meals and as a place for the family to gather, and the floor to both sides was covered with branches, straw, or the like for sleeping.

In such ways, although there were neither interior walls nor doors, the pit dwelling came to be divided up according to use, with a clear-cut functionalization of space.

It may be deduced that this functionalization led, from the mid-Yayoi period onward, to the establishment of a more or less fixed style. It became normal to arrange four pillars in a square in the interior, and it appears that beams were placed atop these pillars and joined by sloping timbers to form the roof truss.

In large part, such advances were made possible by the spreading use of chisels, adzes, and other iron tools.

The Transition from Village to "State"

As a consequence of the rapid rise in agricultural productivity, and of rice in particular, the villages of the Yayoi period gradually combined into federations that could be called "states" (*kuni*). The period during which this happened, from the fourth into the sixth centuries, is known as the Burial Mound period.

The Chinese history *Chronicles of the Three Kingdoms* (ca. A.D. 297) says the following about third-century Japan: "Formerly more than one hundred states ... Now, thirty maintain intercourse through envoys." As this suggests, the smaller states were gradually being absorbed or consolidated to form larger states representing entire regions of the country.

In order to increase agricultural productivity, the leaders of larger states would bring weaker states under their rule, mobilizing the labor resources they represented to bring rivers under control and carry out the irrigation and water-control works necessary in creating paddy fields. To achieve this, the leader must inevitably have possessed enormous power. At death, he or she was buried with a degree of ceremony appropriate to that power and authority, and a huge mound was erected over the grave. It is from these mounds that the name of the period is derived: the Burial Mound period.

The construction of these burial mounds, or tumuli, required the same formidable amount of labor as the opening of new paddy fields. The largest, traditionally thought to be the tomb of the emperor Nintoku, has a keyhole shape, is 486 meters long and 35 meters high, is surrounded by a moat, and covers 32.3 hectares. Some 20,000 funerary *haniwa* (clay models and figures) are estimated to have been originally placed on the surface. The four basic shapes of these mounds are round, square, front-square and rear-round (the keyhole shape), and front-square and rear-square. Particularly impressive examples of the latter two types were built in the fourth century in the Yamato district of the Nara

■ Village in the Burial Mound Period

basin and at the foot of the hills of the Kinai district around Osaka.

Eventually, the small states of the Kinai area (which is roughly equivalent to present Nara prefecture) were to join together to form the state of Yamato. The date when this occurred is not certain, being ascribed to either the late fourth or early fifth century. A major spur to this event was provided by people from the Korean peninsula, who brought with them a wide range of advanced technology. This technology embraced agriculture and civil engineering as well as sophisticated techniques for making iron, pottery, and woven materials. It served not only to raise productivity in the Yamato state as such,

front-square rear-
round burial mound

raised dwelling

smoke outlet

but to give an impetus to the unification of the country as a whole.

In the sixth century, in the Asuka district where the court of the Yamato state had its seat, cultural elements brought from the continent began to bear fruit on local soil. The "Asuka culture" was predominantly Buddhist in tone, and unlike the other areas that still adhered to the old Burial Mound culture, the making of Buddhist images and temples spread rapidly among the aristocracy.

Since it would have been difficult to build large temples with existing architectural techniques, master carpenters were invited from Paekche on the Korean peninsula. In contrast to ordinary dwellings, whose pillars were embedded directly in the earth, these temples were built on solid stone podiums. Their pillars rested on base stones, their eaves were supported by a complex system of brackets, their roofs laid with tile, and their wooden surfaces embellished with color and metal fittings.

It took a considerable time for the technology employed by the Yamato state to spread to outlying areas, but as agricultural productivity increased, various styles other than the pit dwelling appeared among the housing of local leaders.

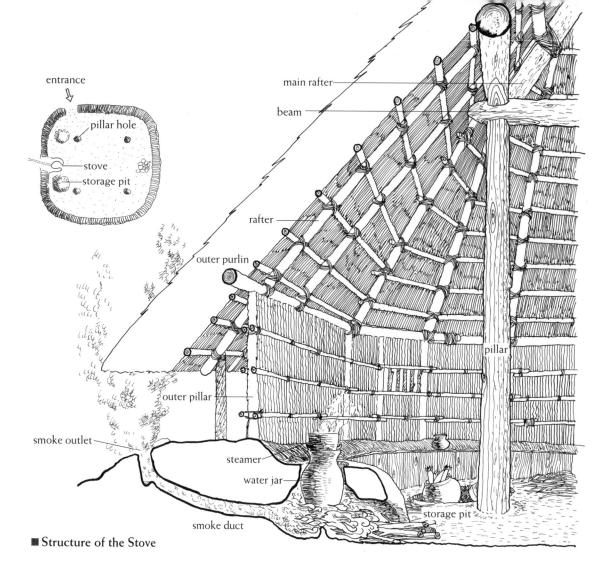

entrance

pillar hole

stove

storage pit

main rafter

beam

rafter

outer purlin

pillar

outer pillar

smoke outlet

steamer

water jar

storage pit

smoke duct

■ Structure of the Stove

Diversification of the Pit Dwelling in the Burial Mound Period

There were several different types of dwellings in the Burial Mound period, but the principal type continued to be the pit dwelling, though its interior underwent further diversification of functional space.

One new interior feature was the earthen stove (*kamado*), which appeared in the latter half of the Burial Mound period. Built next to a wall, the stove was an integral part of the structure, and included an underground duct to convey smoke to the outside. A large water jar was placed on the stove, and on top of it was set a steamer with holes in the bottom. Rice was steamed here, molded into balls, and then put aside for later eating, when they were soaked in hot water.

By the side of the stove, there was usually a storage pit, in which crockery, earthenware containing grain, and so on were kept. The stove and storage pit were usually situated at the farther end of the room from the entrance.

Around the central, earthen-floored section, it became general practice to build a somewhat higher, bunk-like shelf on which straw or rush mats were probably spread for sleeping.

With the stove now installed close to the wall, the danger arose that a low roof might catch fire. Consequently, the main pillars were made higher, and the walls raised up on independent pillars, on top of which rafter-supporting purlins were placed.

Pit Dwelling

The most common type of dwelling from the Jōmon period onward. In the Kinai district, it disappeared by the beginning of the eighth century, but in eastern Japan it was still standard in the Burial Mound period.

Pit Dwelling with Walls

Outer pillars are erected with windows and entrance in between them. Interior space is higher, and the stove is near the wall. In the latter part of the Burial Mound period, this is a common style.

Raised Dwelling

In western Japan, where rice-growing culture first developed, raised dwellings appeared at an early date. In the Burial Mound period, there were fine specimens with open or railed verandas for the ruling class.

Raised Storehouse

Appearing in western Japan in the Yayoi period, the raised storehouse was also built in eastern Japan by the Burial Mound period.

Ground-level Dwelling

The ground-level dwelling that began to appear around the seventh century, chiefly in the Kinai district, was rectangular in plan, and the outside pillars had become part of the main structure. There were imposing gables, and the roof ridge was sometimes surmounted by horizontal decorative elements (katsuogi).

Gable-roofed Pit Dwelling

The pit dwelling, whose plan had become rectangular in the Burial Mound period, began to appear with a gable roof and the entrance at the gable end.

■ **Different Types of Dwellings in the Prehistoric Period**

The Raised Dwelling—Symbol of Authority in the Burial Mound Period

In addition to the common pit dwelling, various other types of houses came into being in the Burial Mound period. We know this from relief pictures on the back of a bronze mirror, house-shaped earthenware (*haniwa*; clay models and figures placed on burial mounds), and archeological sites. A major reason for this sudden diversity was that private dwellings had begun to be seen as symbols of social status.

The raised floors hitherto used in storehouses were now incorporated into the residences of local leaders and other high-ranking persons, giving rise to the raised-floor dwelling. The pit dwelling was still the norm, but now a raised-floor dwelling was considered the proper abode for a person of superior status. Such raised dwellings seem to have developed at an early date in western Japan and the central Kinai area, where the rice-cultivating culture was advanced. In the Kantō plain and other areas to the east, however, it appears that, with the passage of time, the ground-level dwelling was most often adopted as suitable to persons of rank.

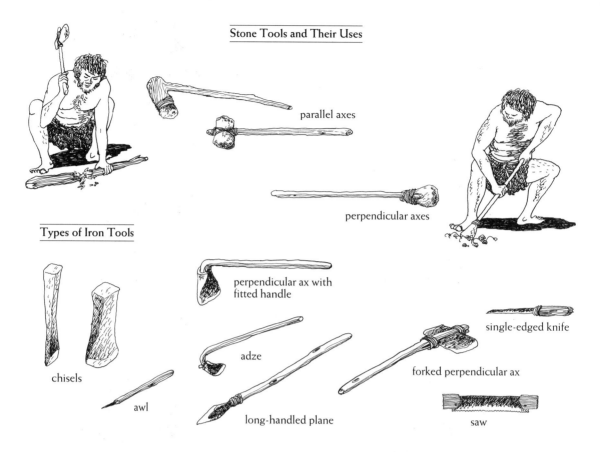

Stone Tools and Their Uses

parallel axes

perpendicular axes

Types of Iron Tools

chisels

awl

perpendicular ax with fitted handle

adze

long-handled plane

single-edged knife

forked perpendicular ax

saw

The Evolution of Building Tools

In the Paleolithic Age and the Jōmon era, the principal building tools had been made of stone. In particular, stone axes with the cutting edge running parallel to the handle were used in cutting wood, and axes with the cutting edge fixed crosswise to the handle were used for digging. However, stone tools had many disadvantages: they wore down easily, they were liable to break upon impact, and they were often heavy. Moreover, the technological development of stone tools was slow.

Around the beginning of the Yayoi period, the building techniques of prehistoric Japan underwent a great change. With the introduction of iron making from the Korean peninsula, iron tools began to be used and wood processing made rapid progress.

The first iron tools to replace their stone counterparts were axes, which had handles that fitted into a metal glove and were thus much sturdier than their predecessors. Iron chisels, too, replaced chisel-shaped stones and were put to a variety of uses.

Long-handled planes (yari-ganna) began to be used to smooth and level the surface of wood from around the end of the early Yayoi period, and they continued in use until replaced in the fifteenth century by bench planes (dai-ganna), which are much like those in use today. The width of the blade was usually from three to five centimeters.

In the Burial Mound period, saws also put in an appearance. Unlike later Japanese saws, they cut on the push rather than on the pull. The cutting edge was only a dozen or so centimeters in length, and they were used for cutting bone or doing small-scale woodwork. From the sixth century onward, such saws were used for cutting across the grain of planks that had being produced by splitting timber along the grain with wedges or chisels.

The Ancient Period

Asuka Period
(590–710)

Nara Period
(710–794)

Heian Period
(794–1192)

The cultural flowering and rise of centralized government that occurred in the Ancient period were based on developments in the Burial Mound period (ca. 300–ca. 590). It was that period that saw the rapid spread of rice cultivation and the establishment of a stable economy. It was then that the Yamato state and its court emerged in the Kinki area and brought rival states under its control. The centralized government that resulted set the stage for what would follow.

In the sixth century, the Yamato state gave birth to a new culture in the Asuka region of Kinai that embodied elements of the cultures of China and Korea. This "Asuka culture" was sustained chiefly by immigrants from Korea, who brought with them, among other things, new systems and technologies and Buddhist culture; they were a major influence in the Yamato court's establishment of central authority.

Perhaps the most significant measure undertaken toward establishing centralized government was the promulgation of the *ritsuryō* code

in the latter half of the seventh century and the early part of the eighth. This system, modeled on those of China and Korea, was designed to give the state a legal framework. All people in areas under the Yamato court's rule were to be recorded in a national register as citizens of the Yamato state, and all land was to become the property of the state. Apparently it was also around this time that the nomenclature for the ultimate ruler of the Yamato court became officially the "emperor" (*tennō*).

As a symbol of the *ritsuryō* system and as a focal point for the bureaucratic machinery centered on the emperor, a new capital was planned, based on continental models, which called for a formal, symmetric pattern of streets and blocks. This plan was first rigorously carried out in the capitals built in Heijō (present-day Nara) and Heian (present-day Kyoto). In contrast to previous capitals, which were more or less temporary sites serving the reign of a single emperor, these two capitals developed into full-fledged cities, acting as political, economic, cultural, and religious centers. Their inhabitants included the imperial court, the aristocracy, bureaucrats, merchants, and craftsmen.

In the Heian period (794–1192), the aristocracy adopted the imposing *shinden* style for their residences, achieving an architectural distinction matching that of Buddhist temples. The merchants and craftsmen, who formed the bulk of ordinary townsfolk, began to build for themselves the combinations of business premises and homes known as *machiya* ("townhouses").

A characteristic of the homes of the Ancient period was the enormous gap between the houses of the aristocratic classes in the capital and those of the farming class. This gap extended not only to ways of living and architectural scale but to building techniques, which belonged to entirely different traditions. The mansions of the aristocracy made use of the sophisticated skills of Buddhist architecture; the homes of the farmers relied on traditional techniques of the type first used in pit dwellings.

The increasingly difficult lives led by the agricultural community in the Nara period and later is indicated in a contemporary poem entitled "A Dialogue on Poverty," in which the author speaks in the voice of a farmer: "Under the sunken roof / Within the leaning walls, / Here I lie on straw / Spread on bare earth, / With my parents at my pillow, / My wife and children at my feet, / All huddled in grief and tears. / No fire sends up smoke / At the cooking place, / And in the cauldron / A spider spins his web, / With not a grain to cook,... / The village headman comes, / With rod in hand,... / Growling for his dues. / Must it be so hopeless—/ The way of this world?" (Yamanoue no Okura: from *The Manyōshū: One Thousand Poems Selected and Translated from the Japanese*. Tokyo: Published for the Nippon Gakujutsu Shinkōkai by the Iwanami Shoten, 1940).

■ Village in the Ancient Period

The *Ritsuryō* Code and the Establishment of Centralized Government

The new centralized governmental system established by the Yamato state was founded on the *ritsuryō* code. The *ritsu* in the term *ritsuryō* signified a penal code, while the *ryō* embraced administrative, civil, and commercial law and various other rules and regulations aimed at exerting control over the land and its people. The system provided for a register of the population, and on that basis paddy fields were allotted to ordinary people, who were in return obliged to pay the Yamato state taxes in the form of commodities and labor.

The country as a whole was divided into provinces and counties, where government offices were set up and court officials dispatched to act

as administrators. Villages were divided, for taxation purposes, into fifty households, each of which consisted of a number of affiliated families.

At first, the lives of farmers were not very different from the Burial Mound period, but as the *ritsuryō* system gradually permeated society, they became progressively harder. This was in part due to the system of taxation. A rice tax required that approximately three percent of the yield be rendered to the state, and from the eighth century onward a further tax was placed on seed rice lent to farmers. Another tax called for cloth to be paid in lieu of doing ten days' annual labor service in the capital, and yet another called for taxes to be rendered in silk, thread, and the like. Corvée labor was an additional burden since it called for unremunerated labor on local public projects for sixty days a year. In addition, soldiers from the eastern provinces (areas north of the Kantō district) were sent down the length of the country to defend the northern coast of Kyūshū against invasion or to serve in the capital as guards at the imperial residence or government offices.

Around the time that the Asuka culture was flourishing (590–710), with temples being built and a well-ordered capital constructed using corvée labor, the pit dwellings of the farmers were becoming progressively smaller and more cramped. A further reduction in size during the Nara period (710–794) and on into the Heian period (794–1192) clearly shows that farmers no longer had the means even to built decent homes.

bamboo slats

main rafter

beam

thatch foundation

purlin

exposed wattle window

embedded pillar

mats over earthen floor

earthen floor

stove

water jar

chip box

■ Interior of Farmer's Home

From Pit Dwelling to Ground-Level Dwelling

Around the time that capitals were being established at Asuka and then Heijō (Nara) and the country was being unified under the *ritsuryō* system, the dwellings of farmers, especially in the central Kinai district, underwent a gradual change. The use of pillars, beams, and other techniques of wood construction developed to the point where it was possible to erect a free-standing house with outer pillars only, doing away with the inner pillars seen in earlier dwellings (compare the illustration above with that on p. 24). The pit was also eliminated.

Even in the Kantō district, far from the capital, pit dwellings were being built without erecting interior pillars by the latter half of the ninth century. These houses hastened the eventual change to ground-level dwellings.

In the culturally advanced Kinai district, the pit dwelling had most likely begun to give way to the ground-level dwelling by the first half of the seventh century and had disappeared completely by around the beginning of the eighth century. It seems likely, though it is not certain, that one of the principal reasons for this was the influx of Korean immigrants who settled in the Kinai district and brought continental forms of housing with them.

In plan, the ground-level dwelling was rectangular. In size, it ranged from two-by-three bays to three-by-four bays, with the length of the bays (the distance between two pillars) being somewhat shorter than was usual later. It is not certain how the interior was used, but it is believed that it consisted of two rooms, one a bare earthen space (*doma*) and the other of the kind now known as a *doza*, where the ground was strewn with rice husks or straw and then covered with woven mats. There was a stove in the earthen-floored area for cooking.

scoop

chip box for water

water jars

pestle and mortar

flared earthen rice pot

food stand

tray with utensils

movable stove with flared rice pot

baked clay brazier

chip box brazier

stone rosin stand

lamp stands

cabinet

low table

straw cushion

straw stool

wicker basket

wooden clogs

wooden hairpin

comb

two-tiered stand

■ Domestic Articles from the Ancient Period

Articles of Everyday Use in the House

A variety of utensils were used in the houses of the Ancient period, all of them closely related to changes in the style of the dwelling itself. The chief feature of the dwellings of this period was the new and clear distinction made between areas that had a bare earthen floor, a mat-covered earthen floor, and a raised boarded floor.

The nobility came to live in dwellings of the raised-floor type, while even the farmers and the townsfolk began to sleep and eat either on earthen floors spread over with matting or on boarded floors, with an earthen-floored area set aside for cooking and various types of work. As a result, in the absence of the custom of using chairs, the greater part of daily life came to be spent directly on floors of some kind or other, and various articles devised for daily use reflect this practice.

The increase in the variety of cooking and eating utensils, though partly due to an increased diversity in food itself, was also a result of adopting such continental customs as serving food on trays (*zen*) as well as the aversion to putting food directly on the floor, where people walked, sat, and did various types of handiwork. Where heating was concerned, since it would have been impractical to provide each raised-floor room with a sunken fireplace (made by cutting a hole in the floor and fitting it with a box for the fire), various types of movable braziers for burning charcoal or wood proved convenient. Charcoal, of course, was hard to come by, so in most cases firewood was used.

Lamp stands, on which saucers of oil with wicks were placed, were also intended for life on the floor, though the vegetable oil used as fuel was, like charcoal, beyond the reach of ordinary people. Shelves and low tables gradually came into use as a way of keeping the floor area uncluttered; seldom-used objects were stored in cupboards, chests, and baskets located in the corners of the room.

Life in the Heijō and Heian Capitals

The old Japanese word for "capital" (*miyako*) meant "the place where the imperial palace is." It was the site of the homes not only of the emperor and his family but also of persons serving at the court. It was the custom at first for a "capital" to remain the capital for the reign of only one emperor, and to be reestablished elsewhere with the enthronement of a new emperor. However, from the enactment of the *ritsuryō* system onward, Japan began to follow the examples of China and Korea in establishing a permanent capital, which was to be based on a symmetrical grid pattern. After several false starts, this type of capital was fully established with the Heijō capital (present-day Nara) and the Heian capital (present-day Kyoto), which was to remain the capital from 794 to 1868.

The grid pattern consisted of a checkerboard of numbered blocks known as *jō*, which ran from north to south, and *bō*, which ran from east to west. A broad street called Suzaku Avenue went down the center of the grid. At the northern extremity of the avenue, facing south, was the imperial palace. Government officials were provided with residential land within the capital in accordance with their rank. Temples and markets to the east and west of Suzaku Avenue were also established.

Of the several capitals built according to this plan (see p. 35), including Heijō and Heian, all were alike in that they centered on the imperial family and government officials; they were, indeed, "the place where the imperial palace is." This is particularly apparent in the structure of the grid plan, including the fact that the city was divided into two halves, called the Right Capital and the Left Capital, as seen from the imperial palace at the north end of the city. Still, insofar as the capital had to provide the essentials of daily life, it was also a consumer city, and markets were provided to meet this need.

In the Heijō capital, the east and west markets were run by officials known as "supervisors,"

■ Townhouses in the Heian Capital

and "market people" were licensed to maintain the stores. The market people are thought to have belonged to mid-ranking and lesser clans in the surrounding Kinai district who controlled the production of commodities, and in this sense were different from the merchants of later periods.

It was not until Heian became the capital that merchants and artisans who could be called townspeople began to make independent livings within the capital. In Heian, as in Heijō previously, markets were established and commodities were supplied by market people, but an increase in

population also encouraged the emergence of independent merchants. Goods essential to everyday life were brought in from agricultural communities on the outskirts of the capital, commodities submitted as taxes by outlying districts began to circulate in the capital, and commercial activities became increasing lively.

The dwellings of the merchant and craftsman class were known as *machiya*—"townhouses"—but it is not certain whereabouts in the Heian capital they were actually located. Contemporary sources such as picture scrolls suggest that the townhouses were situated in the outlying

districts in the vicinity of the markets or lined the back streets. These townhouses were small—the front facing the street was from one-and-a-half to two bays, and the depth only three to four bays. Their goods were displayed on a stand placed outside the house.

Pillars were embedded directly in the earth, and roofs were shingled. In construction, they comprised a core section (*moya*) and a peripheral section (*hisashi*; see p. 34). They seem to have differed little from farmhouses outside the city. Similar townhouses began to appear not only in the capital but in provincial towns as well.

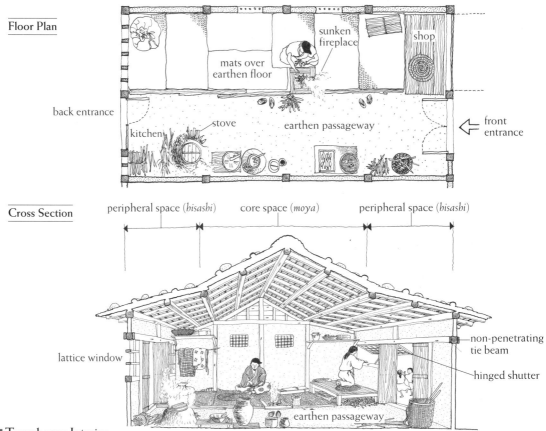

Floor Plan

- mats over earthen floor
- sunken fireplace
- shop
- back entrance
- kitchen
- stove
- earthen passageway
- front entrance

Cross Section

peripheral space (*hisashi*)   core space (*moya*)   peripheral space (*hisashi*)

- lattice window
- non-penetrating tie beam
- hinged shutter
- earthen passageway

■ Townhouse Interior

The Structure of the Heian Townhouse

In the townhouses built in the capital, approximately one bay (or half the width of the house itself) was devoted to an earthen passageway (*tōri-niwa*) running from front to back. Near the entrance of the passageway were kept tools of the trade and stocks of merchandise, while the area at the rear served as a kind of kitchen, with a stove and water jars. The passageway gave onto a back yard where a well, shared with neighbors, was located. The remaining one bay or so of the width of the house was a long, narrow strip of living space. The front part of this served as the shop and had a raised floor on which trade was carried out, while the space behind it probably consisted of woven mats over an earthen floor or a low mat-covered floor of boards resting on logs laid directly on the earth. The roof was usually covered with shin-

gles, and the angle differed between the core (*moya*) and peripheral (*hisashi*) sections. This method of expanding interior space by adding a gently sloping *hisashi* to a more deeply sloping *moya* was a characteristic of the Ancient period in general, and in the Heian period the technique was incorporated into the aristocratic *shinden* style.

The entrance took the form of a hinged wooden door that was suspended from a non-penetrating tie beam. Windows consisted of lattice or hinged shutters backed with paper or the like to keep out wind and rain.

As a class, townspeople living in the capital were not officially recognized and occupied an economically precarious position. As a rule, they lived in simple structures of this long, narrow-facaded type. It is interesting to note that the earthen passageway, which is a feature of merchant dwellings of later periods, already existed in Heian-period townhouses.

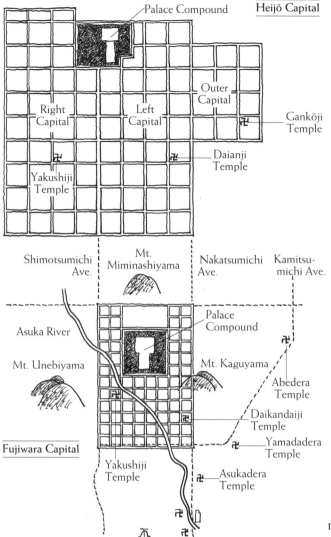

Palace Compound

Outer Capital

Right Capital

Left Capital

Gankōji Temple

Daianji Temple

Yakushiji Temple

Shimotsumichi Ave.

Mt. Miminashiyama

Nakatsumichi Ave.

Kamitsu-michi Ave.

Asuka River

Palace Compound

Mt. Unebiyama

Mt. Kaguyama

Abedera Temple

Daikandaiji Temple

Yamadadera Temple

Fujiwara Capital

Yakushiji Temple

Asukadera Temple

■ The Fujiwara and Heijō Capitals

The Moving and Transformation of the Capital

The capital of the Yamato state did not have a permanent location in the fifth and early sixth centuries, but was moved and reconstructed any number of times. In 645, however, when the Taika reforms were undertaken to establish the *ritsuryō* system, it was felt that a permanent capital should be erected on a Chinese grid pattern to serve as a symbol of the state. The result was the Naniwa capital of 652, which was an attempt

at, rather than a realization of, the planned city. Composed of an imperial palace and other structures devoted to the processes of government, such as the Great Hall of State and the Court of Government, the palace was in a sense the prototype of imperial palaces of later periods. The buildings themselves, however, were still constructed with pillars implanted directly in the ground, rather than resting on the later stone bases, and the roofs were either shingled or thatched, not tiled as they would be later.

The Fujiwara capital, on the other hand, which served three successive emperors from 694 until 710, was based solidly on the Chinese grid layout. Divided up into a checkerboard pattern of twelve east-west and eight north-south blocks, it was the first example of town planning in Japan. The Court of Government, which had pillars standing on base stones and a tiled roof, was the first example of a continental architectural style to be seen apart from Buddhist temples.

The Fujiwara capital made clever use of two long-existing roads—Shimotsu-michi and Nakatsumichi, which crossed the Yamato basin from north to south—as the two main thoroughfares on east and west. Expansion of the city was hampered, however, by hills to the north, east, and west and by a group of ancient burial mounds to the south. In the Heijō capital, to which the seat of government was transferred in 710, Shimotsumichi became the main thoroughfare (named Suzaku Avenue), and the width of the city from east to west grew to twice the size, and the length 1.5 times the size, of the Fujiwara capital. This resulted in three times more space, without even considering the Outer Capital and the additional blocks on the northwest edge of the city.

The Lives of the Aristocracy

During the period during which the capital shifted with each emperor, the palace's central importance was as a symbol of political power. It is unlikely that much consideration was given to the homes of government officials. Almost certainly, their residences within the capital were less splendid than the establishments kept by the powerful clans in the surrounding areas. However, as the capital shifted from Fujiwara to Heijō and then to Heian, several emperors in succession came to rule from one and the same palace, so that government officials and the aristocracy gradually found themselves obliged to move into the capital from their private estates and take up residence on a permanent basis. This is clear from the fact that, in the case of the Fujiwara capital, such people were provided with plots of land in accordance with their rank.

Even so, it seems that the number of those who made a definite move to the capital was, in fact, quite small. Even after the capital moved to Heijō, many of them maintained residences both on their private estates and in the capital itself. Excavations and surveys at the site of the Heijō capital suggest that the structures actually erected on allotted land consisted of a main building and a few secondary structures, with no sign that the master had made a genuine move to the capital with his family and entourage.

Almost all residences of the Nara period made use of ground-embedded pillars; even living quarters within the Heijō palace were built in this fashion. It seems that such dwellings inherited the style of the Burial Mound period more or less unchanged. Most of them consisted of a core area (*moya*) alone. Peripheral areas (*hisashi*) had not yet come into use (see p. 41).

The Heijō capital had little to offer the aristocracy in either economic or cultural terms. Economically, they were still dependent on their estates, while the capital was strictly devoted to matters of government. Culturally, they found

fishing pavilion

■ Aristocratic Residence in the *Shinden* Style

few attractions in the capital, certainly not enough to make it worthwhile settling there.

The situation changed drastically, however, once the capital moved to Heian in 794. As the aristocracy's private estates extended to more distant parts of the country, they naturally found it convenient to establish residences in the capital. Then, as commodities began to flow in from around the country, and as large num-

open corridor

annex

inner gate   gate corridor

Shinden

bers of industrious craftsmen settled in the city, Heian began to function as a true metropolitan center, not merely as the residence of the emperor and seat of government. Government officials and aristocrats alike came to the capital with their families and began to compete in building splendid residences.

It is still not completely clear how the *shinden* style, the typical form of aristocratic dwelling in the Ancient period, came into being, but it seems likely that the emergence of this new city, the Heian capital, provided a major stimulus. One might seek the style's origins in the preceding capital of Heijō or in the influence of the culture of T'ang China, but neither explanation seems entirely adequate.

The Heian Capital and the *Shinden* Style

In 784 it was decided to move the imperial residence from Heijō to Nagaoka, which was to remain continually under construction until 794. At this point, however, a further decision was made to shift the capital to Heian (present-day Kyoto) instead. It was here that high-ranking aristocrats were to take up permanent residence and build mansions in the period-defining *shinden* style.

The layout of the Heian capital followed more or less the same grid pattern as the Heijō capital, but the arrangement of streets and blocks was more clearly defined so as to provide suitable sites for building aristocratic residences. At the outset, only two temples were allowed, one in the eastern half and one in the western half of the city.

The grid employed at the Heijō capital had fixed the distance from the center of one main street to the center of the next at 180 *jō* (1 *jō* equals approx. 3 m.), which meant that any difference in the width of roads produced residential blocks (*bō*) of varying sizes. However, in the Heian capital the unit of measure was taken as one *chō*, which was laid down as 40 *jō*, with the width of the intervening alleys counted separately; hence every block was of the same size.

The area of the grounds of an upper-class residence ranged from one to as much as four *chō*; the minimum plot allotted to ordinary government officials was known as a "one householder" (*hito-henushi*; i.e., 1/32 of a *chō*). This was only half the area allotted in the Heijō capital—a sure sign that the bureaucratic population had undergone an increase.

When the aristocracy began building their residences in the capital, their chosen architectural design was the *shinden* style. The process whereby this style developed is not clear. It seems that at first people had a left-right symmetrical arrangement in mind. In fact, such an arrangement is never found in practice. The reason for this seems to be that the main entrance and rear entrance on east and west created a horizontal axis that

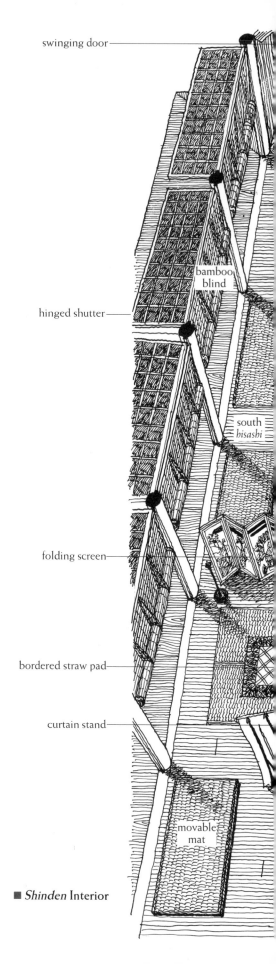

swinging door

bamboo blind

hinged shutter

south *hisashi*

folding screen

bordered straw pad

curtain stand

movable mat

■ *Shinden* Interior

kabeshiro curtain

west *hisashi*

north *hisashi*

two-tiered cabinet

core area (*moya*)

two-tiered shelf

sleeping dais

clashed with the vertical (north-south) axis represented by the main building of the compound, producing an asymmetrical arrangement.

The *shinden* style placed the *shinden* (the main building where the head of the family lived) more or less in the center of the grounds, facing south over a pond and connected by open corridors to annexes to the east, west, and north. From the east and west annexes, "gate corridors" (i.e., corridors with a gate giving access midway along their length to the inner grounds) stretched out to "fishing" and "spring" pavilions, which overlooked the pond.

Near the main gate there were a household office, guardhouse, carriage house, and other structures. Near the rear entrance, situated on the opposite side of the compound, stood the kitchen, ritual affairs office, and so on.

The visitor entered from the main gate, where he alighted from his ox-cart and left his attendants, and passed via an inner gate and the south garden into the *shinden*. The master of the house received guests in the south peripheral (*hisashi*) area, the north peripheral (*hisashi*) area being reserved for everyday living.

The interior of the *shinden* consisted of a core structure (*moya*) flanked by peripheral structures (*hisashi*). The *hisashi* could be built on one side of the *moya*, two sides or four sides, or in a variety of other ways. This created a large, open space, which had to be divided into functional areas by partitions such as folding and single-leaf screens, curtain stands, decorative tapestries, *kabeshiro* walls (curtains with bamboo blinds behind them), and bamboo blinds. These areas were distinguished by such other appurtenances as movable mats, round cushions, straw pads with decorative borders, woven mats, lacquered tables, chairs for ceremonial use, two-tiered shelves, and cabinets.

The *shinden* was the place where the male or female head of the household and his or her spouse lived, while daughters—with or without their spouses—lived in the annexes.

In marriage among the aristocratic class of the day, the man generally went to and from his own home and the woman's, returning to his own home in the morning, a style to which the relaxed layout of the *shinden* style seems to have been peculiarly well suited.

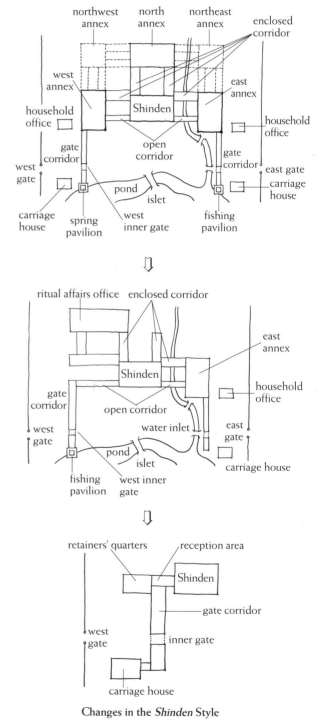

Changes in the *Shinden* Style

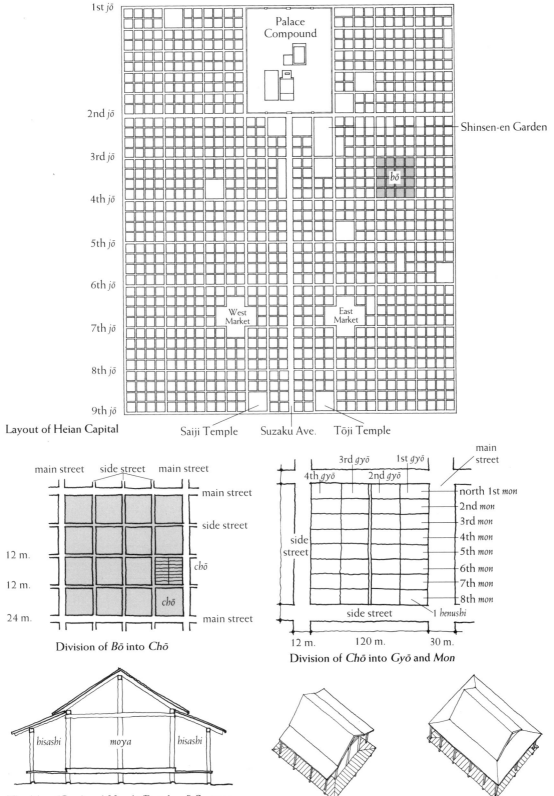

1st *jō*

Palace
Compound

2nd *jō*

Shinsen-en Garden

3rd *jō*

bō

4th *jō*

5th *jō*

6th *jō*

West
Market

East
Market

7th *jō*

8th *jō*

9th *jō*

Layout of Heian Capital

Saiji Temple   Suzaku Ave.   Tōji Temple

main street   side street   main street

main street

side street

12 m.

chō

12 m.

chō

24 m.

main street

Division of *Bō* into *Chō*

3rd *gyō*   1st *gyō*

main
street

4th *gyō*   2nd *gyō*

north 1st *mon*

2nd *mon*

3rd *mon*

4th *mon*

side
street

5th *mon*

6th *mon*

7th *mon*

8th *mon*

side street

1 *henushi*

12 m.   120 m.   30 m.

Division of *Chō* into *Gyō* and *Mon*

hisashi   *moya*   *hisashi*

The *Moya* (Core) and *Hisashi* (Peripheral) Sections

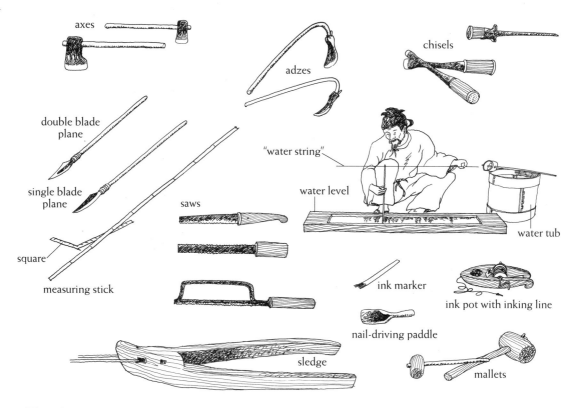

axes

adzes

chisels

double blade
plane

"water string"

single blade
plane

water level

square

saws

measuring stick

water tub

ink marker

ink pot with inking line

nail-driving paddle

sledge

mallets

■ Tools Used in House Building

New Construction Techniques

Construction technology in the Ancient period made great strides forward, with a central role played by the capitals of the Yamato state. Buddhist architecture in particular, brought in by immigrant Korean specialists, introduced a large number of new techniques in wood construction.

Buddhist temples were usually erected on a podium made by compacting the earth; pillars rested on base stones, and roofs were covered with tiles. Color was applied to the pillars and beams, and metal fittings were used as decoration.

Partly because of the social and customary differences between Japan and the continental sources of Buddhist architecture, considerable time elapsed before such techniques were adopted for domestic structures. This began to happen around the middle of the Nara period, and by the Heian period the effects of this technology became apparent not only in the *shinden* style

but also in the homes of ordinary townspeople.

Another factor in the development of building technology, and its dispersion throughout the country, was the Yamato state's incorporation of the construction industry into a centralized organization. Within this organization, experts and workmen were brought together from all over the country and learned the most advanced techniques, such as the use of the sledge to carry heavy stones and the utilization of water levels in keeping ground surfaces and base stones horizontal. When they returned to their home areas, these craftsmen took their newly learned skills with them.

In time, these techniques were adapted for use in dwellings, and sturdily joined beams and roof trusses came to be built, together with walls covered with thick clay. This required increasingly detailed planning and skilled engineering, with a consequent rise in the technical expertise of carpenters, plasterers, and other skilled workers.

The Medieval Period

■

Kamakura Period
(1192–1333)

Muromachi Period
(1333–1573)

Northern and Southern Courts Era
(1336–92)

Warring States Era
(1467–1573)

Momoyama Period
(1573–1603)

■

The Medieval period was characterized by the permanent transfer of political power from the court to the military class or samurai. That first occurred when the warrior Minamoto Yoritomo displaced the aristocracy to become the foremost power in the land. This marked the beginning of the Kamakura period, in which the nation was overseen by a supreme military commander (*shō-gun*) and his government (the shogunate).

The Kamakura shogunate was supplanted in 1333 when two important vassals turned against it. In the ensuing Muromachi period, another military regime, the Muromachi shogunate, continued previous policies and developed new ones in an attempt to consolidate its position, but its control over provincial samurai was weak from the beginning and grew increasingly so as time passed. Two sub-periods often distinguished are the Northern and Southern Courts era, in which two rival imperial lines fought for legitimacy, and the concluding Warring States era,

when provincial warriors (*daimyō*) fought against one another, and against the Muromachi shogunate, for political domination.

The period was decisively brought to an end when the warrior Oda Nobunaga toppled the Muromachi shogunate and gained control of the country. This event marked the beginning of the Momoyama period. With Nobunaga's death, his chief subordinate, Toyotomi Hideyoshi, followed in his footsteps until his own death, when Tokugawa Ieyasu emerged victorious from a brief period of internecine fighting. The period in which he and his descendants ruled supreme is known as the Edo period.

When the Kamakura shogunate was first established in 1192, the nation's political center shifted from the capital of Heian (present-day Kyoto) to Kamakura, which until then had been no more than a remote village in a distant eastern province. Throughout the Ancient period, the center of power had always been situated in the Kinai district, and the creation of this new center of government was an unprecedented event. Nevertheless, the city of Kyoto continued to be the economic and cultural center, and its traditional aristocratic culture exerted a strong influence on Kamakura and other samurai-dominated provincial towns. This included aristocratic dwellings and lifestyles, which continued to center around the *shinden* style.

At the same time, a new type of culture introduced from China was to become the spiritual mainstay of the samurai class: the culture of Zen Buddhism. Many elements of the Zen way of life, in both its spiritual and material aspects, were to be taken up by the samurai and made their own.

Gradually, a number of objects not found in traditional culture came to be adopted into samurai dwellings. This included features of the *hōjō* (the quarters of the abbot of a Zen temple) and its garden; the customs of tea drinking and associated ways of entertaining guests; and hanging scrolls bearing a painting or calligraphy, writing implements and their accessories, and the other objects referred to collectively as *karamono* ("Chinese things"). All of these were adopted by the samurai, and little by little they brought about changes in the *shinden* style, gradually breaking down fixed notions about the house and permitting a greater degree of creative experiment.

Private Estates and Manor Lords

The *ritsuryō* system of the Ancient period was based on the principle that all land was owned by the state, but from the Nara period (710–794) onward the system gradually decayed as private, non-taxable ownership of newly cultivated land was permitted. In particular, from the tenth century onward, powerful provincial families whose lands were taxable vied with each other in "donating" their lands to the non-taxable estates (*shōen*) of the imperial family or the aristocracy, thereby gaining exemption from taxes themselves. In return, they acted as the

■ Manor House of a Private Estate

estate's agents or supervisors and paid tribute to the nominal owners. These estates, in turn, came to acquire freedom from investigation by the provincial and county governors.

From then on, throughout the Medieval period, the estate system was to provide the basis of the nation's economy. In the Kamakura period (1192–1333), the shogunate appointed officials such as military governors and stewards in an attempt to bring these private estates under its control. In the Muromachi period (1333–1573), a system was put into place whereby the military governors were given control of half the tributes of the estates. As a result, farmers within the estates increasingly switched their allegiance from the nominal owner of the estate to the military governor.

Thereafter, the power of estate owners grew progressively weaker. Especially in the provinces of the Kinai district, the base of the imperial family and the aristocracy, the estates tended to

manor house

moat

be taken over by confederations (*gōson*) of middle and small tax-paying landlords. With Toyotomi Hideyoshi's land surveys at the end of the sixteenth century, the private tax-free estates finally disappeared.

Under the estate system, manor lords were members of powerful families with close ties to the land. They were directly served by vassals of whom some were related by blood and some not. These vassals lived both within and without the manor compound, where they played the role of a defensive barrier. Farmers were placed in villages under the lord's supervision on the outer periphery of the compound. The status of some of these farmers was virtually that of slaves.

The manor compound was usually surrounded by a moat or an embankment. Within the moat, the residence itself occupied a central position, together with rowhouses for the vassals not related by blood, stables, storehouses, and so on. Outside the moat lay the residences of the vassals related by blood. Around the manor compound lay the paddy fields directly controlled by the lord of the manor. The paddies and fields of serf-like farmers were usually located in more confined hollows.

At Waki in Izumi province (present Osaka prefecture), there is a site from the early Medieval period. A large-scale manor house was situated within a moat along with dwellings of two units each for the serfs who worked within the compound. The buildings had pillars with stones under their bases to prevent sinking. The size of the main residence was large, basically 3 to 4 bays by 4 to 5 bays, with two or three peripheral sections (*hisashi*). The homes of the household serfs were much smaller, 2 bays by 3 to 4 bays, with no evidence of *hisashi*. Owing to the *hisashi*, the main residence had as many as five or six rooms, whereas the serfs had an earthen-floored space plus, at the most, two living spaces (either mat-covered earth or board-floored).

drying shelf

exposed-wattle window

board floor

mats over earthen floor

dividing beam

earthen floor

■ Interior of a Farmer's House

The Dwellings of the Farmer

R elatively little is known about the dwellings and lifestyles of small farmers or peasants who worked the land of the estates in the Medieval period. Certain conjectures can be made from the Hakogi Thousand Year House (possibly dating back to the fourteenth century) and the Furui Thousand Year House (sixteenth century), which are believed to be among the few surviving examples of medieval farming houses. Other sources are the sites that have been excavated in various parts of the country and the artifacts found at these sites, as well as the houses of the common people depicted in medieval picture scrolls or described in historical documents.

In general, there were most likely still major differences in lifestyle and architectural tech-niques between one part of the country and another in the Medieval period, as there had been in the Ancient period. Nevertheless, it seems safe to say that, overall, the dwellings of the Medieval peasantry were ground-level build-ings without interior pillars.

The dwellings of the relatively affluent usu-ally consisted of one central structure and one or two secondary structures, but the compara-tively small size of the central structures revealed by excavations, together with the fact that little scorched soil has been found in their earthen-floored areas, tends to suggest that the main building and the cooking area were housed under separate roofs. This possibility is strength-ened by the persistence of such an arrangement into the Edo period in the north of Ibaraki pre-fecture and in Tochigi prefecture.

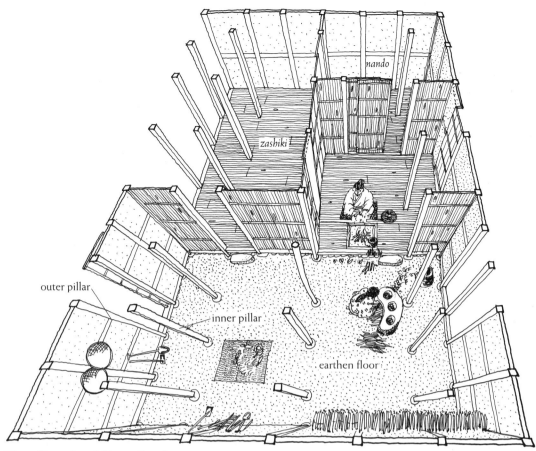

nando

zashiki

outer pillar

inner pillar

earthen floor

■ Floor Plan of an Affluent Farmhouse

The Structure of the Farmer's House

The earthen-floored space of the main structure was large in proportion to the whole,
but it was not entirely made up of exposed earth:
part of it was covered with woven mats and used
as a living space with a sunken fireplace of its own.
A board-floored section seems to have been
used as the sleeping area. This room was located
in one part of the earthen-floored area or to the
rear of the mat-covered room. It was also used
for storing household effects and was thus
sometimes referred to as a *nando* or storeroom.

As for the stove on which cooking (boiling
and steaming) was done, movable stoves had
been commonly used in western Japan since the
Burial Mound period (ca. 300–ca. 590), but in
eastern Japan the sunken fireplace seems to have
been preferred. Built-in stoves probably did not
appear until the end of the Medieval period.

Structures employing pillars thrust into the
ground did not require any special degree of
technical accuracy, but the distance between one
pillar and the next (a bay) was more or less standard for each age. Thus around the Kamakura
period (1192–1333) it was 8 *shaku* (1 *shaku* equals
approx. 30 cm.), in the Muromachi period 7
shaku, and henceforth from 6.6 to 6.3 *shaku*,
becoming progressively shorter over time. The
figure was not always consistent even within the
same house. It varies, for example, in the oldest
extant site, the Hakogi Thousand Year House. In
the later Furui Thousand Year House, the distance parallel to the ridgepole is 6.6 *shaku*, the
distance parallel to the beams 7 *shaku*. Whatever
the length of the bays, the rule was to have a pillar at each interval, with beams extending both
lengthwise and crosswise. Since the beams were
not necessarily straight and their natural curva-
ture had to be taken into account, the pillar tops
usually had tenons to receive the beams.

Medieval Townhouses and the Emergence of Guilds

The city of Kamakura was founded when Minamoto Yoritomo, as we have seen, seized political power in 1192 with the backing of the samurai of the Kantō area. He established his government, or shogunate, in Kamakura in the province of Sagami (present Kanagawa prefecture), far from the Heian capital, Kyoto, where the emperor, court nobles, and aristocracy lived.

Kamakura, as a primarily political city centering around the shogun and his immediate retainers, differed from Kyoto (Heian) in the Ancient period, when Kyoto had, under the leadership of emperor, nobles, and aristocrats, fashioned the nation's government, economy, and culture. Thus even after the political center shifted to Kamakura, Kyoto continued to flourish as the economic and cultural center, a place whose streets were lined with the "townhouses" (*machiya*) of merchants and craftsmen.

An economic turning point had occurred toward the end of the Ancient period among people of inferior status who did various minor jobs for, and supplied goods to, tax-free estates owned by aristocrats, shrines, or temples. In turn, they received protection from the owners of the estates, who were, in effect, their patrons. Eventually these people formed guilds (*za*), which paid a guild tax to their patrons in return for monopoly privileges and exemption from customs duties. The merchants and craftsmen thus organized emerged chiefly around estate markets or in cities such as Kyoto, Nara, and Kamakura, where their patrons lived. Their activities reached a peak in the thirteenth and fourteenth centuries.

Around the same period, a monetary economy developed that filtered down to village society. Even farmers at the lowest level, who had hitherto been subservient to the affluent landlord class, could sell the products from their fields at markets and thereby gain a miscellaneous income and a certain degree of economic

communal well

communal privy

■ Townscape in the Capital

affluence and independence. This led to a large number of markets being held at regular intervals throughout the country.

In Kyoto, there was a district of close-packed townhouses in the Left Capital between Muromachi and Saidōin streets. These were permanent stores or workshops of the kind known as *tana* (lit., "shelves") or *misedana* ("display shelves"). Built to face the street, they shared a yard at the back where there were communal facilities such as a well, a place for drying laundry, a privy, and so on. They were small, their width at the front being usually two bays and their depth about the same. Shelves were put

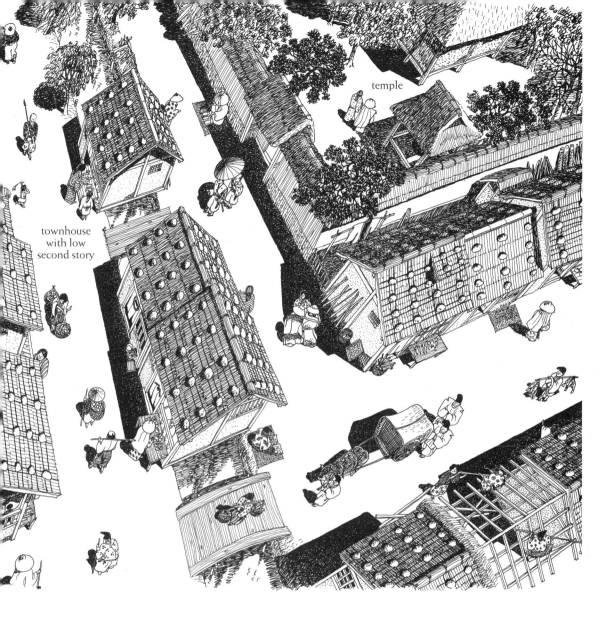

temple

townhouse
with low
second story

out into the street for displaying their wares.

One half of the width of the townhouse was accounted for by an earthen passageway (*tōri-doma*). The one or two living rooms beside it were either covered with woven mats over earth or board-floored. At the back, the earthen passageway gave onto the communal yard, which was treated as an integral part of the dwelling.

On the other hand, in Kamakura—the seat of government—timber workers and other guilds were organized, and the building of townhouses was officially recognized. On the same scale as those seen in Kyoto, they were built in narrow alleyways open at both ends

and had earthen passageways.

Space was scarce in Kamakura, which had hills on three sides and the sea on the fourth, but in similar fashion to Kyoto one *henushi* of land, the minimum area, was allotted to each samurai, the width being fixed at 5 *jō* (approx. 15 m.) and the depth at 10 *jō*. Townhouses seem to have been permitted in seven or eight places near the residences of samurai. Most notable among these was the coastal area at Yuigahama, where breakwaters were built to create a harbor. The result was a bustling commercial district to which large quantities of commodities were brought by boat.

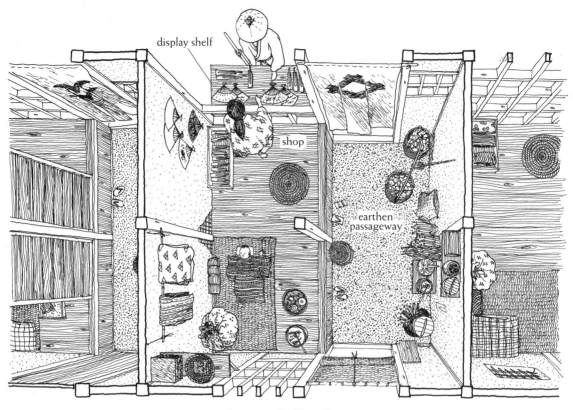

display shelf

shop

earthen
passageway

■ Interior of a Townhouse

The Structure of Medieval Townhouses

Judging from the evidence of picture scrolls and written records, the townhouses of the Medieval period were from two to three bays in both width and depth, somewhat smaller than the average farmhouse in the countryside. It must have been inconvenient to handle commodities for sale and to conduct everyday life in such a small space, but in this respect there was little difference between Kyoto and Kamakura. The probable reason why the houses were lined up in rows with a narrow frontage was that the land on which they stood was rented, and the tax that the landlord paid was determined by the width at the front.

As with farmhouses, the townhouses used pillars thrust directly into the ground, and consisted of an earthen-floored section and living rooms. The latter seem to have been either covered with woven mats over earth or partly board-floored—again basically the same as in the farmhouse.

One area was devoted to a shop, which faced the road and had a display shelf projecting from beneath a latticed window; at night, the display shelf was probably drawn up so as to provide a covering for the lattice. The more valuable articles for sale were shown within the house, and customers came inside to inspect them, so the living space was probably divided into front and rear sections, family life being conducted in the rear. The rear part of the earthen-floored section was used as a kitchen, with a movable stove and cooking utensils. The yard at the rear, which sometimes served as an extension of the kitchen, was provided with a communal well, privy, and space for drying washing. In medieval times human waste was used along with cattle dung as fertilizer, and the communal privies of the townhouses were doubtless a valuable asset to farmers on the outskirts of the city.

clog vender

comb vender

sash vender

oil peddler

rice vender

fishmonger

Marketplace in a Private Estate

A Bathhouse in the Capital

New Businesses Appear in the Cities

As the number of city dwellers increased, various trades and businesses came into being to satisfy needs beyond simple food, clothing, and shelter. This phenomenon became particularly marked as a money economy developed in the middle and latter part of the Medieval period. In Kyoto there were 350 businesses that lent money at high interest rates; in Nara, some 200. These establishments often ran sake-selling businesses as well and amassed considerable fortunes.

Traveling merchants began to bring all kinds of goods into the cities, and various types of entertainers were attracted there. It was almost exclusively in the towns that diversions such as performing monkeys, storytellers, cockfighting, and dancing were to be seen.

Houses of prostitution appeared in certain districts, and bathhouses became common. Bathing was not a general custom at the time, and the bathhouses were used chiefly for the treatment of sickness, but in Kyoto and Nara even the common people began to take steam baths.

Economic activity also began to flourish on a smaller scale in the provincial estates. In most cases, the markets themselves were temporary affairs made up of little more than makeshift shacks. Market guilds took charge of their management, and as the markets began to be held on a regular basis, rows of townhouses began to spring up around them.

Along the Tokaidō highway linking Kamakura and Kyoto, more than thirty post-towns grew up. Besides providing inns for travelers, they attracted goods from the surrounding areas and gradually developed into full-fledged towns.

Samurai Dwellings

Having transferred the political capital to Kamakura, the Kamakura shogunate now set out to vie culturally with aristocratic society in Nara and Kyoto. It proved difficult, however, for the samurai, having long been under aristocratic domination, to create overnight a culture of their own. To a considerable extent, the newly emerging culture of Kamakura was founded on that of the old, court-centered way of life.

The nature of the residences in which the shogun's family and the high-ranking samurai class lived is still not clear, but it is difficult to imagine that they were completely different from the *shinden*-style homes of the Kyoto aristocracy.

In 1333 the Kamakura shogunate came to a sudden end and was replaced by the Muromachi shogunate, which established its headquarters in Kyoto. In this period the dwellings of the shogun's family and high-ranking members of the warrior class maintained the conventions of noble society, and the main elements of their residences carried on the forms of the *shinden* style.

The older *shinden* style did not remain entirely unchanged, but was adapted little by little to the lifestyles of the medieval warrior class. In a sense, this was a period of transition to a new mode of living.

In the *shinden* style, the core area (*moya*) and south peripheral area (*hisashi*) had been used since the end of the Ancient period for formal and ceremonial occasions, while the north *hisashi* and "extended *hisashi*" (*hisashi* added to *hisashi*) were used for the family's everyday living. The division between the south and north sections was marked by translucent screens fitted in separate grooves and by swinging doors (*tsumado*). Though this style remained basically the same in Kyoto during the Kamakura period, there was change in that the north *hisashi* was expanded and further subdivided by screens and partitions of various kinds, with new distinctions made between different areas for private use.

■ A Samurai Residence

During the Muromachi period, the *shinden* style remained almost unchanged where the more formal aspects of everyday life were concerned. This included such structures as the main gateway, the "inner gates," the gate corridors, the carriage shelter, and the guardhouse. At the same time, various facilities intended more for family use began to be built, including such separate apartments as the *tsunenogosho* for the master's daily activities and the *kaisho* for informal gatherings, along with others such as the *jibutsudō* (a room housing a personal object of worship or ancestral tablets) and the "spring pavilion," which overlooked the pond. The *kaisho* was often a single room or a temporary space in another structure, but in the shogun's

residence it developed into an independent building under a separate roof. When gatherings were held in the *kaisho*, it was tastefully decorated with paintings, ceramics, and other objects imported from China, which in turn created a need for interior furnishings such as decorative recesses, staggered shelves, and built-in desk alcoves.

Apart from upper-ranking warriors residing in the capital, a majority of the samurai of the Medieval period lived in rural communities, where their vassals were close at hand. Their residences were surrounded by a moat and an inner embankment, with the master's dwelling in the center. Even though there were no formal ceremonies of the aristocratic type, their residen-

tial compounds followed a simplified form of the *shinden* style, having short, projecting "gate corridors" and the southern and northern sides devoted, respectively, to the reception of visitors and the daily life of the family.

As to marriage customs in samurai society, a transformation occurred from around the end of the Ancient period into the beginning of the Medieval period. The customary practice changed from the acceptance of the husband into the bride's family to the acceptance of the bride into the husband's family. From then onward, the normal family living under one roof consisted of the head of the family and his wife, together with the son and heir with his wife.

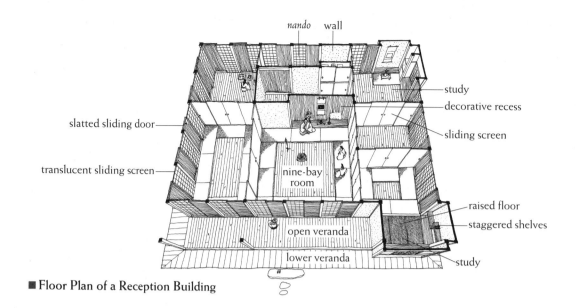

nando   wall

study

decorative recess

sliding screen

slatted sliding door

translucent sliding screen

nine-bay room

raised floor

staggered shelves

open veranda

lower veranda

study

■ **Floor Plan of a Reception Building**

The Beginnings of the *Shoin* Style

The Muromachi period saw the beginnings of a new style of architecture among the samurai class that was to have repercussions down to the present day. This was the *shoin* style. In its final form, this style's chief characteristics were to be the convoluted nature of its interior space—with formal areas, family areas, kitchen, etc. being clearly demarcated—and the furnishings that came to distinguish the formal rooms.

One of the changes that occurred in the Muromachi period that suggested future events was the de-emphasis of the ceremonial aspect of life in favor of private family life. Under this new emphasis, the *tsunenogosho* in the north peripheral area (*hisashi*) of the *shinden*, formerly the private room of the head of the household, became the most important room and was used for the private entertaining of guests. In residences of the shogun, where there were large numbers of visitors, it was sometimes housed in a separate structure.

In the residences of the upper echelons of the samurai class, a simplified form of a *shinden* annex, known as *kogosho*, was sometimes built as a separate structure for the everyday activities of blood relations.

In another change of emphasis, the *kaisho* (see p. 52) came to be built as a drawing room specifically for the entertaining of private family guests. In the residences of the shogun, several *kaisho* were sometimes accommodated in separate structures for use in gatherings involving large numbers of visitors. Where the *kaisho* was constructed separately (see illustration above), the reception space was separated by decorative sliding screens into rooms for different purposes. The room known as the *kokonoma* ("nine spaces"; so called because it measured three bays square) was reserved for the most distinguished visitors and had a decorative recess (*oshiita*; the forerunner of the *tokonoma* or decorative alcove) on the side opposite the entrance, in which a picture scroll was hung.

These semi-private rooms, all having their specific functions, were partitioned off by double-grooved sliding screens, either covered with decorative cloth or paper (*fusuma*), overlaid with translucent paper (*shōji*), or paneled. Use of such screens meant that square pillars were more suitable than round, and these gradually became general. Cushions for sitting and other furniture became permanent fixtures, as did fitted *tatami*—either exclusively around the outside of the room or completely covering the floor—along with such decorative features as the *oshiita* (decorative recess), staggered shelves (*chigaidana*), and the *tsuke-shoin* (built-in desk alcove).

Decorative recess (precursor of decorative alcove)

Shelves (precursor of staggered shelves)

Desk recess (precursor of built-in desk alcove)

Door to sleeping quarters (precursor of decorative door)

Zashiki Fittings and Their Formalization

In samurai residences and Zen Buddhist temples in the latter part of the Medieval period, it became common practice to provide rooms known as *zashiki* with various decorative appurtenances ("*zashiki* fittings") in accordance with their respective functions. The *zashiki* (lit., "laying down a cushion for sitting [on wooden floors]") was a room that was to undergo various permutations throughout its history, but essentially referred to a room for formal use that had thick, fitted straw mats (*tatami*) laid wall to wall. It was to become one of the quintessential features of the Japanese home, even though its function was not always clear or fixed. In large part, "*zashiki* fittings" appeared in samurai residences and Zen temples because they were needed for the display and appreciation of articles imported from China, including books, hanging scrolls bearing Buddhist or other paintings, writing implements, and tea utensils, which were part and parcel of the Zen culture introduced in this period.

The decorative recess known as an *oshiita*, which seems to have been the predecessor of the modern *tokonoma* (decorative alcove), was a shallow boarded space in front of which a low table was placed bearing the *sangusoku* ("three appur-

tenances")—flower vase, incense burner, and candlestick. It was seen chiefly in rooms used for entertaining. When there were guests, a Buddhist painting would be hung on the wall behind the *oshiita* and flowers arranged in the vase.

The shelves were used for storing or displaying scrolls, tea bowls and utensils, and the like. Shelves used for storage were known as *todana* ("door shelves"), those for display as *chigai-dana* (staggered shelves). The "staggered shelves," so called because of the irregular arrangement, took various forms and usually occurred in conjunction with the built-in desk alcove (*tsuke-shoin*).

The latter was a miniature study made by extending one part of the room out onto a well-lit veranda and fitting it with a writing desk and translucent screens. Later, there appeared the *hira-shoin* ("flat desk"), which had a translucent screen as a window but did not project onto a veranda.

What was known as the *nando-gamae* or *chōdai-gamae* was originally an arrangement created by raising the threshold and lowering the lintel to the entrance of the room used for sleeping, with bolts installed on the inside of the wooden door as a means of ensuring personal safety or the safety of valuables. The raising of the threshold was originally intended to keep in the straw spread on the floor, but later became a regular, decorative feature of the *hiroma* (to be discussed later).

Medieval Building Techniques and Craftsmen

The dwellings of the Medieval period were far more varied and esthetically satisfying than those of the Ancient period. This was due largely to the efforts of medieval craftsmen.

Under the *ritsuryō* system of the Ancient period, there were various organizations that engaged, as public undertakings, in work on temples, shrines, and imperial and aristocratic residences. Among these were the Muku-ryō (Woodworking Bureau), Takumi-ryō (Carpentering Bureau), and Shuri-shiki (Office of Repairs). With the collapse of the *ritsuryō* system, these organizations gradually withered away, to be reorganized under the medieval estate system.

In order to secure their positions and stabilize their livelihood, the craftsmen of the Medieval period began to obtain from the lords of the estates who requested their work—their "patrons"—special recognition as official carpenters qualified to work on projects such as temples. In return, they were expected to provide free labor or gifts of money or goods. In Nara, where many great temples were seeking to restore the fortunes of the older sects of Buddhism, this system is evident as early as the end of the thirteenth century, but in Kyoto, where the traditions of the old *ritsuryō* organization were stronger, it appeared somewhat later, in the fourteenth century. In the provinces, this system came into being in the fifteenth century. This status of official carpenter was inherited by successive generations of one, or several, families, and since the construction of large temples and shrines was generally undertaken by guilds, this usually meant inheritance by leading members of the guilds.

The work of the craftsmen of the middle ages involved working principally in wood, but various other specialist trades also emerged—tilers, shinglers, plasterers, smiths, copper work-

long-handled plane

adze

■ **Medieval Carpenters at Work**

ers, and so on.

As the Medieval period emerged from the internal strife of the Northern and Southern Courts era (1336–92) and entered the fifteenth century, the estate system gradually began to crumble from within. In time it gave way to a system in which government was decentralized, with local lords (*daimyō*) ruling each his own domain. In the confederations (*gōson*) of middle and small tax-paying landlords that appeared within the estates, agricultural production increased, bringing relative affluence. Surplus

measuring stick

water level

"leaf" saw

tool box

chisel

square

ink pot with inking line

produce began to be put on sale, and regular markets came to be held at post-towns, ports, and other places. Against this economic background, the skilled craftsmen began to find work to do in outlying villages and provincial towns as well. Those chiefly responsible were the master carpenters (*tōryō*), who made available to the provinces the skills and techniques hitherto exclusive to the seats of government.

From the fifteenth century onward, these master carpenters effected revolutionary changes in building techniques. The appearance of the two-handled ripsaw made possible a plentiful supply of boarding, and the newly invented bench plane was introduced to provide a good finish. The master carpenters increased efficiency by employing diagrams and prenumbered pillars; proportional standards or modules were set for structural parts to achieve overall architectural harmony; and building work began to be contracted out at predetermined rates. The master carpenter, in short, laid down the pattern for the building of dwellings throughout the coming Edo period.

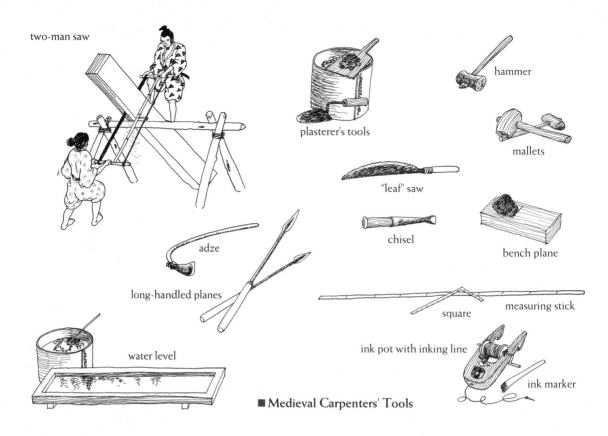

two-man saw

plasterer's tools

hammer

mallets

"leaf" saw

adze

chisel

bench plane

long-handled planes

water level

square

measuring stick

ink pot with inking line

ink marker

■ Medieval Carpenters' Tools

New Tools—The Two-Man Ripsaw and Bench Plane

During the first half of the Medieval period, from the Kamakura period (1192–1333) on into the Northern and Southern Courts era (1336–92), the older building tools underwent almost no basic change, including saws used for cutting at right angles to the grain (*nokogiri*), chisels (*nomi*), long-handled planes (*yariganna*), adzes (*chōna*), axes (*ono*). From the fifteenth or beginning of the sixteenth century, however, two new tools led to a great leap forward in design and building technology.

First, the appearance around the middle of the fifteenth century of the two-man saw (*oga*), which cut along the grain, greatly facilitated the processing of timber, and in particular of boards, which hitherto had been a rare commodity. Until then, timbers had been processed by splitting a log with a chisel and then using an

adze or long-handled plane to finish it, but with the appearance of the new ripsaw it became possible to produce boarding with comparative ease for ceilings and walls. This type of saw was used by men working in pairs, and craftsmen appeared who specialized in its use, but in the Momoyama period (1573–1603) there also appeared a variation of this saw (*maebiki-noko*) that could be used by one man working alone.

The bench plane (*dai-ganna*) that was invented toward the end of the Medieval period proved extremely effective in smoothing boards sawn using the two-man saw, and its use spread rapidly. While it would seem that this plane, as with the two-man ripsaw, came to Japan from abroad—from China or Korea—the Japanese plane is pulled rather than pushed as it is elsewhere.

These two tools became indispensable in building the homes of the upper classes, which were designed according to finely specified proportional standards and modules.

The Edo Period

If the Medieval period was the age of the samurai, the Edo period was the age of the commoner, as lowly farmers and merchants gradually came to assume the most influential role in society.

Having unified the country and put an end to the confused civil strife

that characterized the end of the middle ages, the Tokugawa shogunate—the military government set up by Tokugawa Ieyasu—established a system in which the country was ruled primarily by the shogunate itself and secondarily by feudal lords, with Edo (present-day Tokyo) as the center of power. Owning vast territories throughout the country, the shogunate placed under its allegiance the whole of society, from the court nobility and the great temples and shrines to the lords (*daimyō*) of the feudal domains. In broad terms, the shogunate divided society into four classes: the samurai, the farmers, the craftsmen, and the merchants. Furthermore, it took advantage of its policy of national seclusion to gain control over the whole of the nation's markets.

While the new order gave society a new stability and productivity, it also had the revolutionary effect of drawing the traditional agricultural communities into the commodity market. It also simultaneously promoted urban life in the castle towns and elsewhere, encouraging the accumulation of wealth by the very merchants who, ironically enough, were eventually to impoverish the finances of the feudal lords.

These were the developments lying behind the remarkable flowering of merchant-class culture known at its height in the Osaka-Kyoto area as "Genroku culture" (after the Genroku era of 1688–1704) and in Edo as "Bunka-Bunsei culture" (after the Bunka and Bunsei eras of 1804–31). The Genroku-era author Ihara Saikaku, in his *Japanese Family Storehouse* (*Nippon eitaigura*; 1688), painted a vivid picture of the nation's merchants. He described the magnificent premises of Daikoku-ya, one of Kyoto's great stores, but also mentioned a fabulously wealthy merchant who lived in rented premises with a meager two-bay frontage, and another merchant of Sakata in the north who started by running a humble inn and ended up as a rice dealer with premises measuring thirty bays wide and sixty-five bays deep.

In Edo, merchants from the Osaka-Kyoto area began to set up branches known as *edo-dana* ("Edo shelves") and vied with one other for the patronage of the shogunate and the provincial lords, who were obliged under the shogunate's *sankin-kōtai* system to maintain establishments in Edo as well as in their own territories. Then, around the middle of the period, native Edo merchants also entered the field. The merchant families built their shops and storehouses in the fireproof *dozō* or *nuriya* styles, but for the personal, residential areas of their establishments they preferred the *shoin* style used in samurai-class dwellings or the *sukiya* style influenced by tea-room architecture. Although there were strict shogunate ordinances prohibiting extravagance in the building of merchants' homes, the residential premises concealed behind their business establishments were often substantial in size and lavishness.

In the same way, farming families in the countryside, particularly those occupying official village positions, often accumulated considerable wealth by selling fertilizer, brewing sake, running pawn shops, and such like. They built themselves correspondingly luxurious homes, with the emphasis that was placed on receiving visitors seen in the way that the formal *zashiki* incorporated elements of the *shoin* style, such as decorative alcoves, staggered shelves, and "built-in desks." The type of house often referred to nowadays as "traditionally Japanese" is a product of the lifestyles of the Edo period.

Village Life and the Farming Community

When the Tokugawa shogunate seized power early in the seventeenth century, it faced a number of problems concerning the farming population, which had their roots in the Medieval period. In the latter half of the fifteenth century, military governors had taken charge of provincial estates, consolidated powerful local families, and became themselves, in some cases, the lords (*daimyō*) of an extensive area. They were to be succeeded by the so-called warring-states *daimyō*, who secured control over even more extensive territories during the civil wars at the end of the Medieval period. Confronted with a bewildering succession of rulers, the peasants attempted to secure their autonomy and rights by means of organized uprisings known as *ikki*.

Coming to power in 1603, the Tokugawa shogunate sat about establishing a system that would ensure its control over the agricultural community. First, it forbade the farming population to possess weapons or relocate to other areas, thus creating a clear social distinction between them and the samurai, who could possess weapons but must now live in towns, preventing them from forming seditious ties with the farming community. It also established a system whereby the theoretical rice yield of a particular piece of territory was fixed in terms of *koku* (a measure equivalent to 180 liters of rice), based on the area of the paddies, dry fields, and manorial grounds. Yearly tribute, miscellaneous taxes, and corvée labor were determined by income in terms of *koku*.

The village was composed, first of all, of the registered tax-paying farmers (*hon-byakushō*) who owned paddies, dry fields, and residences, and were responsible for seeing that tribute was duly paid. Under them worked various categories of people who were, in effect, serfs with few rights. Serf holders consisted of powerful local families indigenous to an area since medieval times and a powerful class of farmers who considered themselves descendents of the first pioneers of the locality. From among these, one was appointed as village headman (*nanushi*; also known in various areas as *shōya* or *kimoiri*),

■ Village Headman's Residence

a post that in many cases was inherited within the same family. He was assisted in his duties by a "group leader" (*kumi-gashira*) who was in charge of financial matters, while the tax-paying farmers as a whole were represented by a villagers' representative (*hyakushō-dai*). These three officials together were responsible for village affairs in general.

In the early part of the Edo period, the feudal lords of outlying domains sought means of increasing their tributary income. New paddies were created and irrigation improved, tax-paying farmers were encouraged to form tax-paying branch families, and serfs were urged to set themselves up as independent tax-paying farmers.

If a village should suffer from successive poor harvests, the burden of the annual tribute and the obligatory corvée labor would become difficult to meet. This led villagers to form mutual aid organizations and cooperate in such work as the building and rethatching of one another's homes.

As the commodities market of the towns gradually permeated the rural communities from the middle of the Edo period onward, farmers within the villages themselves began selling everything from fertilizer, sake, *miso*, and soy sauce to oil and sundries, and artisans such as carpenters, smiths, and coopers also appeared. Having little cash income, the farmers began to take advantage of the winter season and other intervals in the agricultural calendar to earn money by taking firewood and charcoal, vegetables, wheat flour, and buckwheat flour to sell in the towns. At the same time, however, an increasing number of farmers had to sell their fields under a burden of debt, or to quit agriculture altogether, so that the gap between rich and poor in the villages grew ever wider.

Cases occurred of village headmen being expelled for failure to pay the required tribute, and other headmen were replaced annually as a matter of policy. On the other hand, some of the village headman class accumulated wealth by running pawn shops or selling fertilizer and began to build "rowhouse gates" (*nagaya-mon*) and formal-style entrances (*shikidai*)—both of which were, in theory, permitted only in houses of the samurai class. The development of marked regional differences in farmhouses is a reflection of such trends in agricultural communities.

The Farmhouse and the *Hiroma*

There is still insufficient information as to how the dwellings of the agricultural communities in the Edo period changed and developed from those of medieval times. What is clear is that in the seventeenth century, with the beginning of the Edo period, farmhouses grew considerably larger than those of even the landlord class in the latter half of the Medieval period, and the technology employed to build them had become increasingly sophisticated. A major reason for this development was the stabilization of the livelihood of the tax-paying farmer, but it seems likely that another underlying factor was the rapid advance made in carpentry techniques and their spread to the provinces from the fifteenth century onward.

In the early part of the Edo period, the pillars of farmhouses came to be set on base stones planted in compacted earth, and were firmly held in place at their base and summit by a crisscross arrangement of sturdy beams. The arrangement was further strengthened by tie beams passing through the pillars. Walls were plastered or boarded, with sliding wooden shutters or translucent screens for doors and windows. In order to support the thick thatched roof, a system of separate main pillars and side pillars connected by a framework of beams was used.

The arrangement of rooms was in the *hiroma* style, with one very large main room (*hiroma*) in the front and a *zashiki* and a *nando* for sleeping purposes at the rear. This arrangement became common nationwide, almost as though it were a symbol of the tax-paying farmer's growing independence.

At the sunken fireplace in the *hiroma*, the head of the family sat in the most distinguished place, with his back to the decorative door and decorative recess. His wife's place, with her back to the floor-level sink, was also considered important, since it was she who supervised the household finances.

hiroma

■ Farmhouse Interior

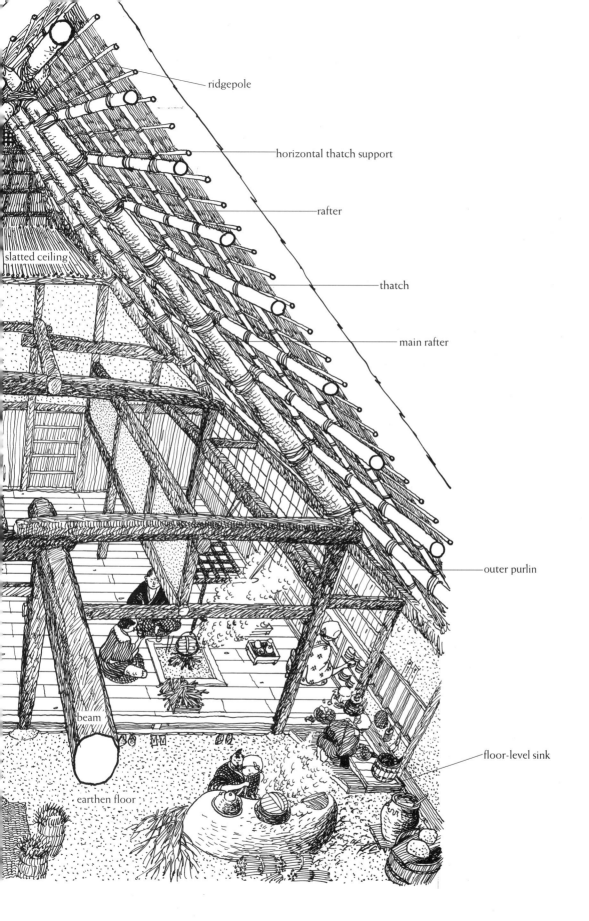

ridgepole

horizontal thatch support

rafter

slatted ceiling

thatch

main rafter

outer purlin

beam

floor-level sink

earthen floor

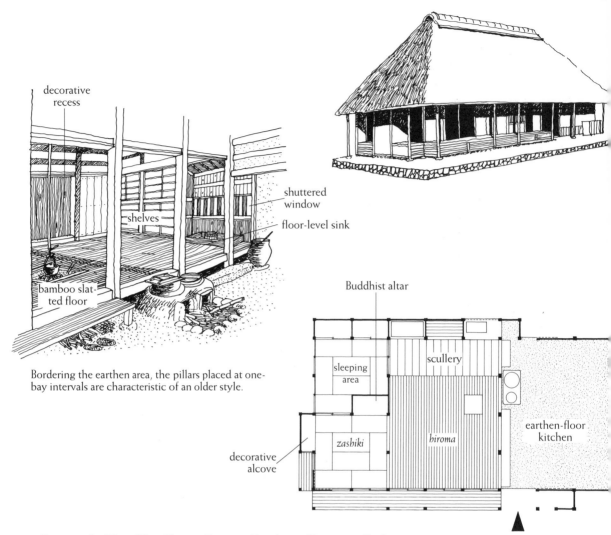

decorative
recess

shelves

bamboo slat-
ted floor

shuttered
window

floor-level sink

Bordering the earthen area, the pillars placed at one-
bay intervals are characteristic of an older style.

Buddhist altar

sleeping
area

scullery

zashiki

hiroma

earthen-floor
kitchen

decorative
alcove

■ Rectangular Floor Plan: Former Kitamura Residence, Kanagawa Pref.

Regional Variations of the Farmhouse (1)

Rectangular Floor Plan (*Sugoya*)

The farmer's dwelling of the Edo period took definitive form around the middle of the seventeenth century as the livelihood of the tax-paying farmer stabilized. Subsequently each district developed its own characteristic style in keeping with the natural surroundings and other special characteristics of the area. Despite regional differences, however, the basic form was still that which came into being in the early Edo period.

In that period, pillars thrust directly into the ground gave way for the most part to pillars resting on base stones, and the scale of the building as a whole became considerably larger. The floor, too, which had formerly consisted of woven mats over earth or at most of boards placed over logs resting directly on the earth, increasingly became a raised floor—notably in the bedroom and *zashiki*. The usual number of rooms in the homes of petty farmers was three, with one large main room (*hiroma*) plus a *zashiki* and a bedroom (*nando*). In the Kinai district, some houses had four rooms to accommodate more visitors, but in all cases the basic plan was rectangular.

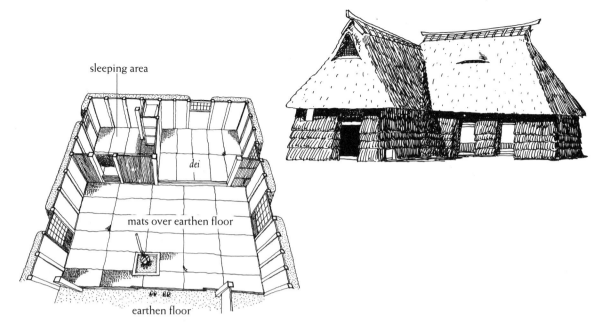

sleeping area

dei

mats over earthen floor

earthen floor

The two pillars implanted directly into the earth at the edge of the earthen area are relics of medieval practice.

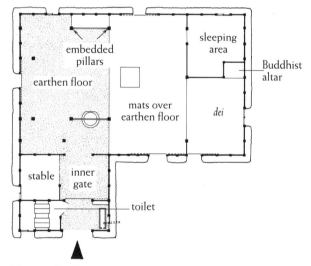

embedded pillars

earthen floor

sleeping area

Buddhist altar

mats over earthen floor

dei

stable

inner gate

toilet

■ Thatched-wall House: Former Yamada Residence, Nagano Pref.

The Thatched-Wall House

On the plains, the walls of farmhouses were mostly of earth or clay, but in the hills where timber was plentiful and ripsaw artisans numerous, board-walled houses were also built. However, making boards was time consuming and expensive, so in remote villages with heavy snowfalls many houses were built with thatched walls, which were effective in retaining heat and keeping out rain and snow.

The house whose plan is shown above was originally in Akiyama Village in a remote part of Nagano prefecture. The floor plan, which is in the *chūmon* style (see p. 67), shows the influence of the Niigata area. There are few openings to the exterior, and the *nakanoma* room follows the older *doza* style of having woven mats over an earthen floor.

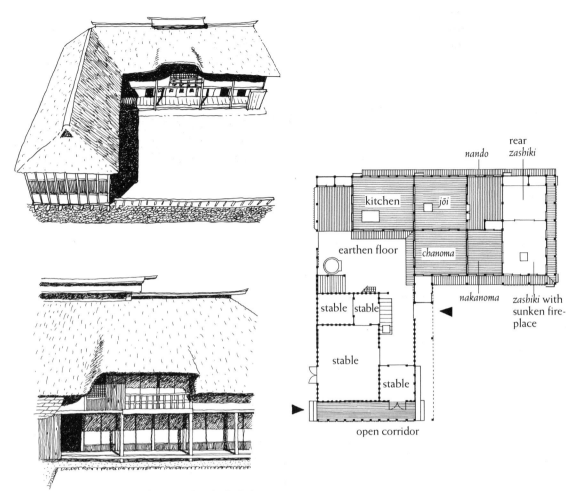

nando

rear
zashiki

kitchen

jōi

earthen floor

chanoma

stable | stable

nakanoma

zashiki with
sunken fire-
place

stable

stable

open corridor

The second floor area, under the unusual roof called a *kiriya*,
is used by the oldest son and his wife as a sleeping area.

■ L-shaped Floor Plan: Former Chiba Residence, Iwate Pref.

Regional Variations of the Farmhouse (2)

L-shaped Floor Plan (*Magari-ya*)

A *magari-ya* ("bent house") is a farmhouse in which a stable has been joined to a rectangular main building (*sugoya*; see p. 64) to form an L-shaped structure. This type of dwelling is found on both the Pacific and Japan Sea sides of northern Honshū.

The Nanbu district of Iwate prefecture, in particular, is distinguished by the large number of *magari-ya* found there. It seems that stables were originally separate from the main structure, but came to be integrally connected with it in an L-shaped pattern as a result of the local feudal domain's policy of encouraging the rearing of horses. The entrance is located in the earthen-floored part (*doma*) of the annexed section, which made it possible to keep an eye on the horses while working in the *doma*.

The L-shaped structure is also found in the north of Ibaraki prefecture, the west of Chiba prefecture, and the east of the Tokyo metropolitan area, but the annexed section in these cases consists of an ordinary *doma* or *zashiki*, not stables.

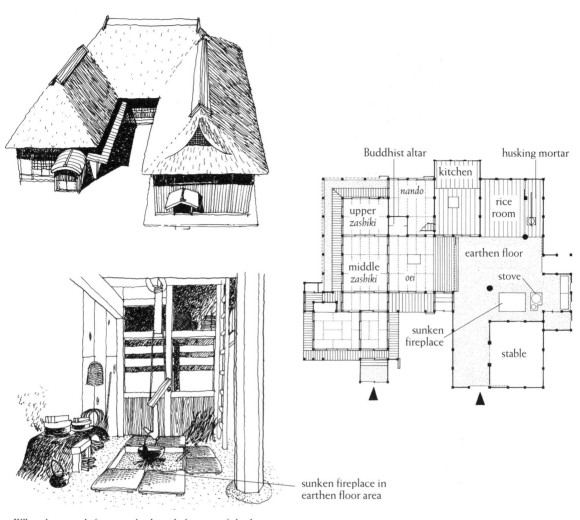

When busy with farm work, the inhabitants of the house ate around this fireplace without bothering to go up into the raised-floor interior.

■ *Chūmon* Floor Plan: Former Nara Residence, Akita Pref.

Chūmon Floor Plan

The *chūmon* style is found on the Japan Sea side of Honshū from Niigata prefecture to Akita prefecture. In plan, it somewhat resembles the *magari-ya*, but the projecting section both serves as a passageway to the living quarters and houses the stables, privy, and storeroom.

This style is considered to have been developed to facilitate entry and exit in times of heavy snowfall, but in some cases the *zashiki* and kitchen are included in an additional projecting wing to form an inverted U-shape, the whole of which is called a double *chūmon*. In others, an extra wing is added at the back ("rear *chūmon*" style), and in still others an additional stable is annexed, the result being called the "stable *chūmon*" style.

Both the *magari-ya* and the *chūmon* styles traditionally had three rooms including a *hiroma*, but later the four-room pattern became general. The four-room arrangement had been in use from a much earlier period among wealthy local families.

main rafter

silkworm room

purlin · beam

living area

The slope of the roof is much steeper than usual in farm-houses, partly to prevent the settling of snow and partly to take full advantage of the loft thus created.

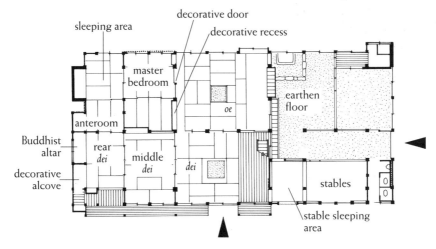

sleeping area

decorative door

decorative recess

master bedroom

oe

earthen floor

anteroom

Buddhist altar

rear *dei*

middle *dei*

dei

stables

decorative alcove

stable sleeping area

■ *Gasshō* Style: Murakami Residence, Toyama Pref.

Gasshō Style

The *gasshō* ("hands raised in prayer") style is found in Gifu prefecture at Shirakawa and on the upper reaches of the Shō River, and in the Gokayama district of Toyama prefecture.

The style came about in order to permit extended families to live together and raise silk-worms indoors in remote hilly areas with heavy snowfall. A huge, steeply sloping roof was con-structed, with the space beneath the rafters divided into two or three levels by slatted floors for rearing silkworms. The gabled entrance per-mitted easy access to the building in time of heavy snow.

The *gasshō* styles in Gokayama and Shirakawa differ in that Gokayama houses have the en-trance on the gable side (*tsuma-iri*) and have a large earthen space, while those at Shirakawa are entered on the non-gable side (*hira-iri*) and have almost no earthen-floored space.

The house belonging to the Murakami family at Gokayama (see above), which was built around the middle of the Edo period, is clearly divided into *zashiki* at the front and family living quar-ters at the rear. The *oe*—a local name for the room first encountered inside the entrance—has a sunken fireplace and typical *zashiki* fittings such as a decorated door, a decorative recess, and shelves.

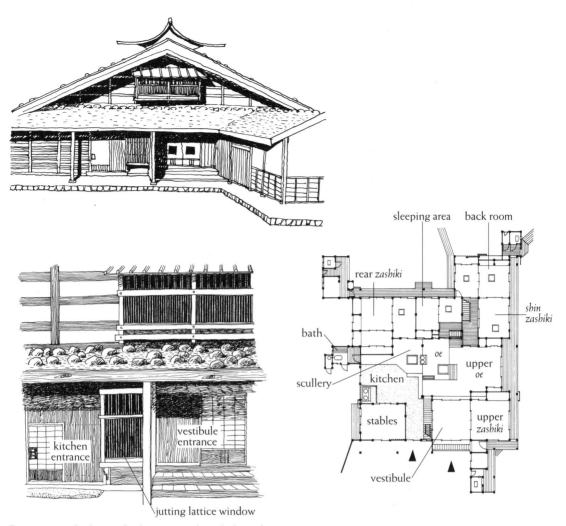

sleeping area   back room

rear *zashiki*

shin
zashiki

bath

oe

scullery

upper
oe

kitchen

stables

upper
zashiki

vestibule

jutting lattice window

Facing a main highway, this house served as a lodging for feudal lords and other important personages on their way to and from Edo, which explains the attention paid to the details of the facade.

■ *Honmune* Style: Horiuchi Residence, Nagano Pref.

Honmune Style

In the *honmune* style, a gently sloped roof is covered with shingles, which are weighted down with stones. The gable side, where the entrance is, presents an impressive appearance with its tie beams and jutting lattice windows, and at the peak of the bargeboards is an ornament of the type known as *suzume-odori* ("sparrow dance") or *suzume-odoshi* ("sparrow scarer"). Farmhouses in this style are found throughout Matsumoto-daira in Nagano prefecture.

In the plan of the Horiuchi residence (see above), the *oe* is centrally placed, with a *zashiki* for entertaining guests near the entrance and, at the rear, sleeping areas and subsidiary *zashiki*. This distinguished style, which reached its final form in the middle or latter part of the Edo period, was permitted only to officials of the village. Since the Horiuchi family were wealthy overseers (*ōjōya*), there is a formal entrance (*shikidai*) to the right of the regular kitchen entrance.

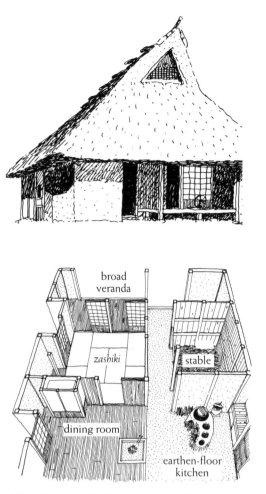

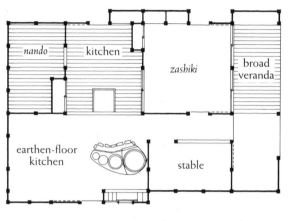

The wide veranda, facing south, was used for various purposes, including receiving everyday guests and doing handiwork.

■ *Tsuma-iri* Style: Former Izumi Residence, Osaka Pref.

Regional Variations of the Farm-house (3)

Tsuma-iri Style

The *tsuma-iri* ("gable entrance") style, generally believed to be older than the *hira-iri* ("side entrance") style, is found in several areas from the Kinki district to the Hokuriku district. There are a number of types.

One, known as the "Nose type," is found in an area from Nose at the northern extremity of Osaka to the east of Hyōgo and at Nishiyama in Kyoto. It divides the house vertically into two parts, one an earthen-floored section (*doma*) and the other a section for living in (see for-

mer Izumi residence, above). The *doma* contains a stable and a cooking stove, while the living quarters have a *zashiki* next to the broad veranda at the front of the house, a "kitchen," and a *nando*. Later, the number of rooms in the living quarters of this style increased from three to four.

In the Yogo area north of Lake Biwa in Shiga prefecture, there is a style known as "Yogo." This arrangement consists of two rooms plus a *hiroma*. The living room (*niuji*) leads off the earthen-floored area (*doma*) and is floored with woven mats spread on a layer of rice husks. Beyond it lie the bedroom and the *zashiki*, side by side. This style is also found in Ishikawa and Aichi prefectures.

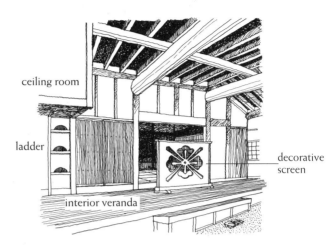

ceiling room

ladder

decorative screen

interior veranda

The interior veranda is a sign of this house's high status. Climbing the ladder on the left leads to a room suspended from the ceiling.

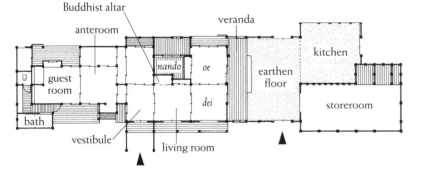

Buddhist altar

anteroom

veranda

guest room

nando

oe

kitchen

earthen floor

dei

storeroom

bath

vestibule

living room

■ *Takabei* Style: Yoshimura Residence, Osaka Pref.

Takabei Style

In the *takabei* ("high wall") style, the fringe around the outer edges of the thatched roof is covered with tile, and the gable is filled in with plaster to create a "high wall." The overall effect is one of gradual steps up the structure to the peak of the roof. This imposing style was one of those used by powerful local families around Osaka and Nara from the early part of the Edo period.

The Yoshimura family were local overseers (*ōjōya*) of Minami-Kawachi. Their residence (see above) was surrounded by a moat and a wall, with a rowhouse gate (*nagaya-mon*), paired storehouses (*narabi-kura*), and a public notice board. The section of the main building to the right of the vestibule constituted the family's living quarters, and that to the left was devoted to entertaining guests, the two being completely separate.

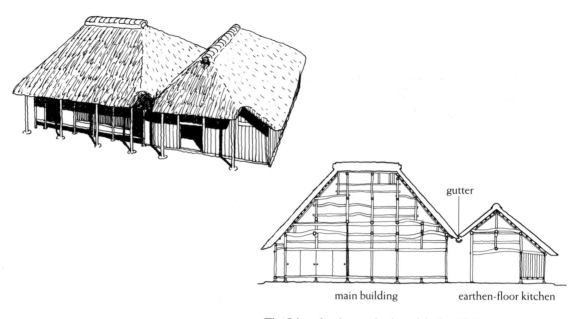

gutter

main building   earthen-floor kitchen

The Sakuta family were leaders of the local fishing community, and the earthen area was made large enough to accommodate a boat and other equipment.

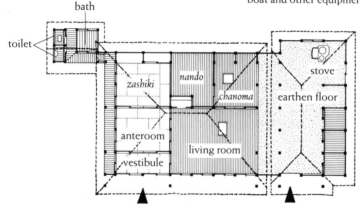

bath

toilet

zashiki   nando

chanoma

anteroom

living room

vestibule

stove

earthen floor

■ *Buntō* Style: Former Sakuta Residence, Chiba Pref.

Buntō Style

In the *buntō* ("separate roofs") style, the main building with the family's living quarters and the wing with the cooking stove and *doma* (earthen-floored area) are housed under visibly separate roofs, the whole forming a single dwelling.

This type of house is found over a wide area extending from Okinawa to the Amami islands, Kagoshima, Kōchi, and areas of the Pacific coast of Honshū from Aichi to Shizuoka and from the Chiba peninsula to the northern part of Ibaraki prefecture. In recent years its existence has also been confirmed in the inland area of Tochigi prefecture.

There are two types: one where there are two completely separate buildings (found in Okinawa), and another where the two are joined at the eaves and the interior spaces form a single whole. The reason that this particular style developed is not known, but one possibility is that since these areas are frequented by typhoons, an attempt was made to minimize the possibility of fire breaking out by positioning the kitchen section so that the ridge faced into the wind.

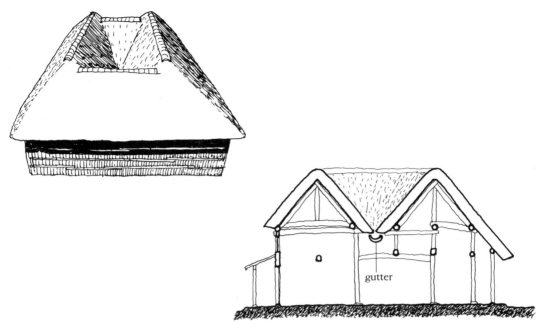

Rainwater gathers in the gutter and is carried away via a drainpipe inside the building.

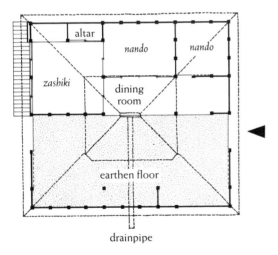

■ *Kudo* Type: Yamaguchi Residence, Saga Pref.

Kudo Type

In this type of house, which is found from Saga prefecture on into Fukuoka and Kumamoto prefectures, the roof plan forms either an inverted U or a hollow-square shape. Typhoons are frequent in this area, and it was once thought that the purpose of having two low roofs, instead of one high one, was to reduce wind resistance. Later, however, it was learned that the style evolved from a rectangular plan to which a two-bay wing was added for a *zashiki*, creating an L shape; then another two-bay wing was added at a later date for the *doma*, creating an inverted U shape. Each wing had a facade of two bays because the domain stipulated that this be the width for projecting wings. The hollow-square shape developed at a later date.

Development of the Castle Town

During the Warring States era toward the end of the Medieval period, contending feudal lords (*daimyō*) began to construct new castles to strengthen their positions. Rather than being built in mountainous areas as had been done previously, these castles were constructed in flatlands, where the castles could serve as economic and communication centers. With the castle as the focal point and symbol of authority, feudal retainers and merchants took up residence in the surrounding area and a town developed. Among the Tokugawa shogunate's measures aimed at keeping the feudal lords under control was the decree that there should be only one castle to each domain. Thus domanial castle towns, not to mention Edo itself, were organized and developed as centers of politics, trade, and communications.

Arranged immediately around the castle were the residences of the lord's retainers (see pp. 82–83), and outside these were the dwellings of craftsmen, merchants, and other commoners. These dwellings were usually organized into districts (*machi* or *chō*) according to the trades of their occupants. This is the origin of such placenames as Daiku-machi (Carpenters' District), Sakan-machi (Plasterers' District), Kaji-machi (Smiths' District), Tatami-machi (Mat Makers' District), Nabe-machi (Pot Makers' District), Tenma-chō (Post-horses' District), and Sakana-machi (Fishmongers' District).

In principle, townspeople were allotted land at the discretion of the lord of the castle, but they had the freedom to buy and sell the right to use it. According to their relationship to land and property, townspeople were classified into landowners (*jinushi*), houseowners (*iemochi*), land tenants (*jigari*), and shop tenants (*tanagari*). Only landowners and houseowners were allowed to participate in the administration of their districts.

In addition to a district (*machi*) tax, townspeople were required to pay a public tax levied

■ View of Town from the Castle

on houses and shops according to the width of the frontage, a national tax imposed on craftsmen, and miscellaneous ad hoc taxes imposed by the local lord. Even so, the burden was comparatively light compared to the tribute that farmers had to pay.

Each district was administered by a local magistrate (*machi-bugyō*), whose chief duties consisted of conveying directives from the shogunate, carrying out various censuses of the population, seeing to the public peace and measures for coping with fires and other disasters, and maintaining and repairing water supplies, bridges, other public facilities.

Public installations of the district included a *jishinban*, a kind of office staffed in rotation by the houseowners of the district, which dealt with public affairs on behalf of the magistrate. It was also the headquarters for the police and the fire brigade. In the Kyoto-Osaka area, the *jishinban* was known as the *machi-kaisho* and doubled as a hairdressers (*kamiyui*). There was also a wooden gate (*kido*), which was the official gate-

way installed at the entrance to each district. Another form of shogunate control, it was supervised by a gatekeeper installed in a nearby watchman's station (*ban-goya*). The gate was regularly closed at 10 P.M., and it was the watchman's job to let latecomers in through a small door off to one side.

Initially, merchants were intended to be cogs in the consumer economy of the samurai class—the rulers of the castle town—and as such were officially responsible for providing all kinds of services and goods. From the middle of the Edo period onward, however, the merchant class eventually gained dominance over the samurai in economic matters.

The economic plight of the samurai was exasperated by the system of *sankin-kōtai*, whereby provincial feudal lords (*daimyō*) and their retainers had to spend alternate years in their domains and in Edo, leaving their wives and children in the city as virtual hostages. Instituted by the shogunate as a security measure, this system saddled the samurai with huge expenses.

Because of this influx of feudal lords, Edo was not only the castle town of the Tokugawa family, but also the site of residences (classified into primary, secondary and tertiary) of the provincial *daimyō* and their retainers. This meant that seventy percent of the land was occupied by the samurai, whereas that held by the merchant class was a mere thirteen percent, even though both classes numbered about 500,000 people.

In the latter half of the Edo period, the number of townsmen in Japan's two great cities, Edo and Osaka, swelled rapidly. Large businesses and stores in the imposing *dozō* and *nuriya* styles (see p. 77) lined the main thoroughfares, while the side-streets were full of dwellings for coopers, mat makers, and day laborers, who lived and worked on the premises, in addition to smaller stores selling sundries, cheap sweets, and so on. The typical dwelling of the common townsperson was the rowhouse (*nagaya*), which was a row of individual apartments under one roof (see pp. 79–81).

fire lookout

machi office

fire tower

machi gate

main street store

night watch man's station

■ Main Street Townscape

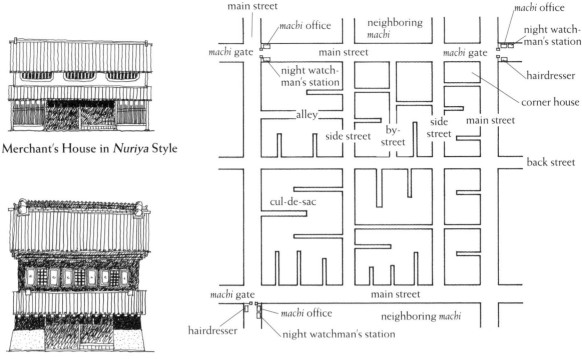

Merchant's House in *Nuriya* Style

Merchant's House in *Dozō* Style

A Typical Edo *Machi*

Labels in diagram:
main street — *machi* office — neighboring *machi* — *machi* office — night watchman's station — *machi* gate — main street — *machi* gate — hairdresser — night watchman's station — corner house — alley — side street — by-street — side street — main street — back street — cul-de-sac — *machi* gate — main street — hairdresser — *machi* office — night watchman's station — neighboring *machi*

Merchants Flock to Edo

Thanks to the *sankin-kōtai* system of alternate residence between Edo and the feudal domains, many different kinds of merchants and craftsmen came from outlying areas to take up residence in the new metropolis. Particularly in the early part of the Edo period, merchants from Kyoto, Osaka, Ise, Ōmi, and other parts of western Honshū came to sell all kinds of provincial products and to amass huge fortunes into the bargain. They often won the right to call themselves purveyors to the shogunate, official rice dealers, and so on. Their stores (*omote-dana*; "front shelves") faced a main street and combined a business area in the front with a residential area in the rear. The humbler sort of tradesmen, including clerks, craftsmen, and day laborers, lived in back-street tenements known as *ura-dana* ("rear shelves").

The stores-cum-residences set up by Osaka-Kyoto merchants were often more imposing than their main stores back home, but they lacked any uniformity of style. Main-street estab-lishments might have tiled roofs, but back-street dwellings would often have shingled or even thatched roofs. The stores' employees, from chief clerk down to the salespeople and apprentices, had come to Edo without their wives and children, and as a result had very little sense of themselves as citizens of the town.

Frequent conflagrations periodically destroyed large parts of Edo, further diminishing any feeling of local identity. Eventually, as the town expanded and broad avenues and firebreaks were built, a sense of belonging emerged. Local bands of firefighters (*machi-hikeshi*) were formed, and public safety improved in various other ways.

The Plan of a Main-Street Store

The houses belonging to Edo merchants, facing a main street and combining business and living quarters, were usually narrow across the front and deep from front to back. The business premises in the main structure occupied the whole of the frontage, and behind it were

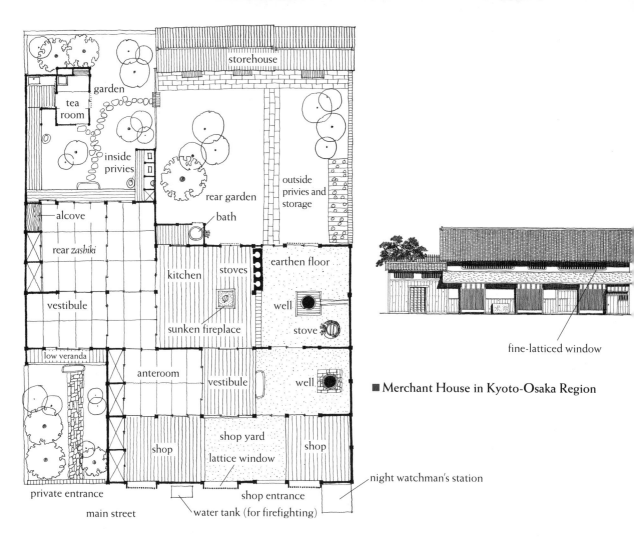

storehouse

garden

tea room

inside privies

alcove

rear *zashiki*

vestibule

low veranda

private entrance

main street

rear garden

bath

kitchen

stoves

sunken fireplace

anteroom

vestibule

shop

shop yard

lattice window

water tank (for firefighting)

outside privies and storage

earthen floor

well

stove

well

shop

shop entrance

night watchman's station

fine-latticed window

■ Merchant House in Kyoto-Osaka Region

various reception and living rooms, a bath room, privy, shed (*naya*), and storehouse (*dozō*). In the larger businesses, with a wide frontage, there was sometimes a wall with a gate for private use; beyond it lay a more formal vestibule and *zashiki* for entertaining.

A typical arrangement in a merchant dwelling had, on one side, an earthen-floored passageway permitting direct access from the main street to the rear, with one or two rows of rooms next to it; this type was often found in the Kyoto-Osaka area. The main entrance opened onto an earthen-floored yard and an adjoining shop; beyond these were the living quarters and reception rooms. In the houses of large businesses, the *zashiki* for receiving guests often had an adjoining garden, with a tea room and other facilities for entertaining in a stylish manner.

In the main-street businesses of Edo, the storefront was usually made up of an earthen-floored area (*doma*) and a board-floored shop area behind it. Customers came into the earthen-floored section and sat on the edge of the raised floor of the shop to be shown the merchandise.

As more and more merchant-class dwellings were built and space became too scarce to allow for wide frontages, two-story houses began to be built. The first to develop was the type known as a *zushi-nikai*, a kind of low second floor at the front of the premises, which was used as the employees' quarters. In time it developed into a regular second floor, where there was a *zashiki* for entertaining visitors. The facade of the second floor took on a variety of forms, making use of such elements of the fireproof storehouse (*dozō*) style as "insect cage" lattice windows (*mushiko-mado*), jutting lattice windows (*degōshi-mado*), and double-hinged (*kannon-biraki*) shutters.

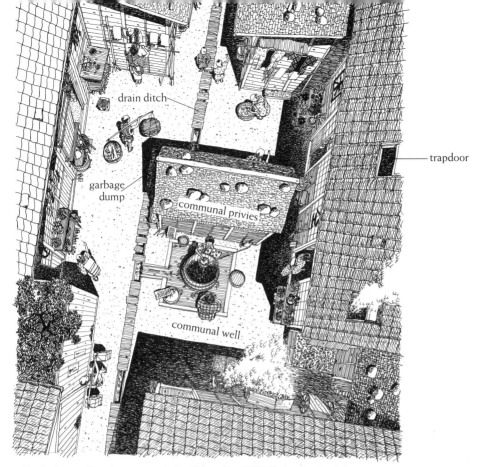

drain ditch

garbage
dump

communal privies

trapdoor

communal well

■ Back-Street Rowhouses and the Communal Well

Life in the Back Streets

Aside from the proprietors of main-street stores, who lived on the premises with their families, the majority of the townspeople lived in the side streets and alleyways behind the main streets. Here were the homes of coopers, sweet-makers, and other craftsmen who worked out of their home, as well as maids, shop clerks, apprentices, small-time merchants, day laborers, and peddlers. In general, their homes were collectively referred to as *uradana* ("rear shelves") in contrast to the big stores-cum-residences on the main streets (*omote-dana*; "front shelves"). The vast majority of these dwellings consisted of rowhouses (*nagaya*; see p. 80). In fact, seventy to eighty percent of Edo townspeople called a rowhouse home.

The entrance to a block of rowhouses had its own gate, which led to a back street or alleyway, a meter or so in width. Down the center of the alleyway ran a ditch to carry away rainwater and kitchen waste water. In some places, the alley widened to form an open space containing the communal well, privies, and a garbage dump, which were under the joint supervision of rowhouse residents.

The landlord or his representative lived in the same block as the rowhouse. He was paid to collect rent on behalf of the houseowner or landowner and had the right to sell the waste from the communal privies to farmers as fertilizer.

The communal well was often the focus of social life, especially among housewives. Aside from the fact that rowhouse residents had to get together to clean it out once a year, the well served as site for doing laundry and preparing for meals. While doing this, housewives would chat with one another and exchange information, holding what was called a "well-side conference" (*idobata kaigi*).

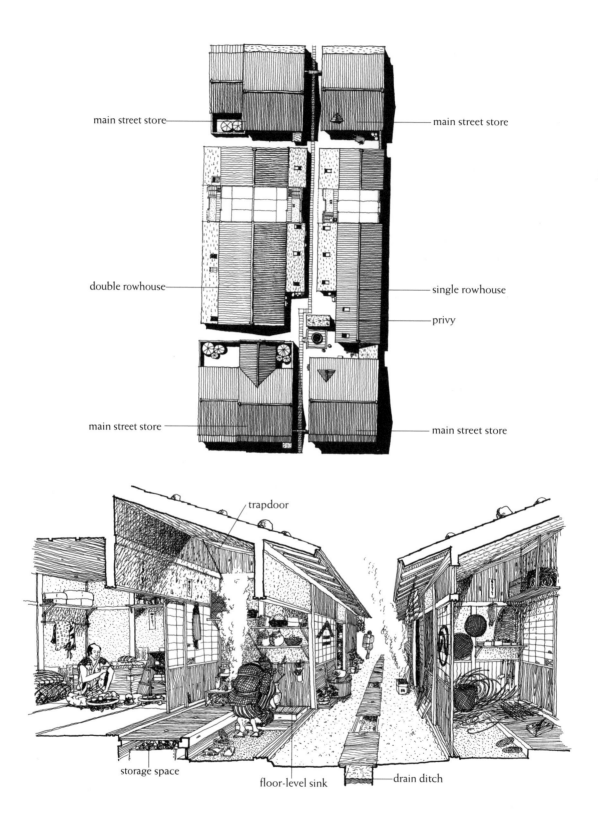

main street store

main street store

double rowhouse

single rowhouse

privy

main street store

main street store

trapdoor

storage space

floor-level sink

drain ditch

■ Positioning of Main-Street Stores and Rowhouses

movable stove
floor-level sink
water jar
drain ditch
drainpipe
earthen floor
potted plant
bench
storage
trapdoor
wainscoted
screen
alleyway

■ Back-Street Rowhouses and Living Arrangements

The Back-Street Rowhouse

There were two types of back-street row-house: the two-row type and the single-row type. In the former, two rows of apartments lay back-to-back under the same long roof, each row occupying half of the width of the building. In the latter, one row of apartments stretched from one side of the rowhouse to the other, thus providing two openings to the outside for sunlight and ventilation in comparison to the one opening for the two-row type. The number of apartments beneath the same roof usually ranged from four or five to ten, though sometimes there were more. The width of one apartment was 1.5 to 2 bays, and the depth 2 to 3 bays.

Rowhouse apartments were usually separated by thin earthen walls, which hardly kept out the smell of cooking, much less human voices. The entrance, facing the alley, had a sliding door with a boarded lower half and a latticed upper half covered with translucent paper. The *doma*

(earthen floor), from which one stepped up into the raised interior, contained the kitchen, with a floor-level sink and a water jar. The step-up between the *doma* and raised interior was about three feet wide and boarded; a trapdoor allowed the space beneath it to be used for storage.

There was another trapdoor in the *doma* ceiling, which could be opened to let out smoke by pulling on a rope. There was just one room at the back, usually of four-and-a-half to six *tatami* mats (one mat is approximately 174 cm. by 87 cm.). At this stage there were no built-in closets of the kind found in most later Japanese-style houses, and *futon* were stored in a corner of the room when not in use. The room not only served as a bedroom and dining room, but was also the place where handiwork was done. *Tatami* mats, wooden sliding screens, and translucent screens were all supplied by the tenant, who carried them with him as personal belongings whenever he moved to new quarters: they were counted, at that time, as valuable private property.

The Castle Town and the Life of the Samurai

Upper-class samurai living in castle towns were allotted land upon which to build their residences, but many restrictions were placed on the land and its use. The size of the land, and of the residence itself, was determined by the owner's status and the size of his stipend (payment calculated in terms of rice from the feudal lord's granary). The higher his rank, the closer he lived to the castle. A man of high rank, such as a "house elder" (*karō*), would manage political affairs from a main residence just below the castle, but he would also be provided, at a farther remove, with second and third residences for everyday living.

In Edo, feudal lords maintained three residences, aside from that in their home domain. The main residence, located in the vicinity of Edo castle, was composed of two parts, one for the lord's official purposes and the other for personal or private use. Among the facilities for formal use were the main gateway, the guardhouse, the entrance hall, the main reception room (*omote-shoin*), and the other reception rooms (*zashiki*). The private area included the quarters of the lord and his wife, kitchens, and the servants' quarters. Facilities such as a Nō stage and tea-ceremony room were provided for entertaining visitors. Positioned around the residence were rowhouses where retainers lived.

The second and third residences, many of which were constructed following the Great Meireki Fire of 1653 for use in times of emergency, were situated outside the outer moat of the castle or on the outskirts of Edo. In practice, they were used as the residences of sons and heirs or vassals, or for the sake of their gardens.

More than 200 feudal lords from all over the country had residences in Edo, and the shogunate supervised the way they lived and all their other activities. Edicts were frequently issued regulating the type of gates at their entrances, the size and style of the buildings, and other

■ Samurai Residence in the *Shoin* Style

such matters, all in accordance with the individual lord's ranking and the income from his lands.

Samurai dwellings were built in the *shoin* style (see p. 84), which reached its definitive form in the early Edo period. The various elements of which it was composed were already in existence toward the end of the Medieval period (see pp. 54-55), but functioned individually and had not yet been organized into a definite style. It

was only as samurai society became fully formed, with its own conventions regulating the entertaining of guests and daily life in accordance with the individual's rank and dignity, that the *shoin* style itself also came to assume its mature form.

Although, as a style of residence, it was in theory only permitted to those of samurai birth, elements of it gradually came to be adopted by increasingly affluent merchants and provincial landowners. There also appeared a less formal variant, influenced by tea-room architecture and known as the *sukiya* style (see p. 85), which gradually spread to the personal living quarters of the samurai, merchant houses, and even to the homes of the more affluent farmers.

■ Interior of a *Shoin*-style Room

The Maturation of the *Shoin* Style

The chief characteristic of the *shoin* style that emerged in the early Edo period was that it brought together, in one room and in a predetermined arrangement, all the decorative elements used in the formal receiving room (*zashiki*) that had hitherto been used haphazardly.

Side by side on the opposite side from the entrance there were a *tokonoma* (decorative alcove) and *chigai-dana* (staggered shelves); on the veranda side of the room there was a *tsuke-shoin* (built-in desk) projecting out onto the veranda (the simplified form, which did not project, was known as a *hira-shoin*, "flat desk"); and on the opposite side from the built-in desk, next to the decorative alcove, were decorative doors (*chōdaigamae*). Another form of decoration was used for *zashiki* where high-ranking guests were to be received. It consisted of raising the level of the floor and covering the adjoining area with decorative molding.

Around the outside of the room was either an exterior veranda or an interior veranda enclosed by translucent screens and sliding wooden shutters. Neighboring rooms were separated by plain or decorated screens. Square pillars were used, and a heavy circumferential rail ran around the room, with a frieze of openwork carving above it. The floor was covered with fitted *tatami*; the ceiling was latticed or battened. The walls were decorated with art work, and in some cases the small areas of wall above the circumferential rail were painted with murals.

Interior partitions consisted of overlapping sliding screens. Sections facing the exterior (see p. 92) had, in the early stages of development, two wooden shutters and one translucent screen running in triple grooves, arranged so that when the wooden screens were pushed back there was half a bay of light. Later this evolved into a combination of two translucent screens, the wooden panels becoming rain shutters running on a single grove so that they could be put away in a box to one side.

This was the form of *shoin* style used in formal reception rooms. In private quarters, the plainer, more relaxed variation known as the *sukiya* style (see p. 85) was preferred, in which the pillars had the bark left on at the corners, the ceilings were battened, the decorative alcove floored with *tatami*, and the decorative shelves subject to variation.

bamboo grill window

crawl door

■ Interior of a Tea Room

The Tea Room

The tea room (*chashitsu*) is a room, or sometimes a small hut, set aside for the performance of the tea ceremony. The ceremony itself, having evolved over a period of several centuries, is essentially a highly structured way of preparing tea in the company of guests, encompassing within itself an appreciation of architecture, gardening, ceramics, religion, history, and spiritual communion.

The form of the tea room was already more or less determined by the late Medieval or early Edo period. As the tea ceremony became an increasingly important element in entertaining guests in samurai society, one room was devoted exclusively to that purpose and became an essential part of the samurai residence. In some cases, it was built adjoining the chief reception room, but it also became fashionable to hold the tea ceremony in a separate, "rustic style" hut built in the garden of a secondary residence.

This "rustic style" tea room, first devised in medieval times by Murata Jukō (1422–1502) and brought to its final form by Takeno Jōō (1502–55) and Sen no Rikyū (1522–91), offered the only opportunity amidst the rigorous formalities of samurai society for host and guests to meet on equal terms. This brief spell of spiritual communion between ranks doubtless came as a welcome relief and form of relaxation. Familiarity with the tea ceremony, as well as with the Nō drama, came to be regarded as essential to the cultivated man, and both acquired a wide following within the warrior class.

A typical free-standing tea room might have *tatami*-covered floors, earthen walls finished with sand, exposed-wattle windows, a bamboo ceiling, translucent and papered sliding screens, a sunken fireplace, and a decorative alcove (*tokonoma*). The entrance (*nijiriguchi*) would be small, only 70 to 80 centimeters high. Overall, the interior of the tea room would be simple and austere.

So-called tea-room architecture (the *sukiya* style) developed from the influence that the tea room had on private residences, inns, and other types of architecture. In contrast to the more stately and flamboyant types of *shoin*-style architecture, it emphasized the use of natural materials (such as posts with bark intact) and freedom in the placement of decorative elements such as alcoves. Though this style developed from within the samurai class, it eventually spread beyond it to the merchants and even the upper levels of the farming community.

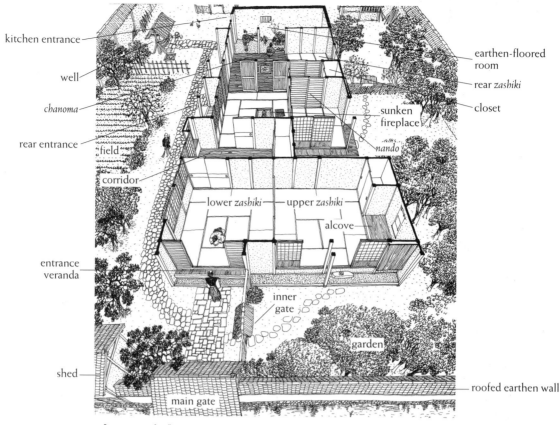

kitchen entrance

well

chanoma

rear entrance

corridor

entrance
veranda

shed

main gate

earthen-floored
room

rear zashiki

closet

sunken
fireplace

nando

field

lower zashiki — upper zashiki

alcove

inner
gate

garden

roofed earthen wall

■ Interior of a Lower-ranking Samurai Residence

The Homes of the Lower-ranking Samurai

Just as feudal lords (*daimyō*) were required to maintain mansions in both Edo and their home domains, the samurai of each feudal lord had to maintain residences both in the local castle town and within their allotted domanial territories, where they installed their own retainers.

These residences, and the lifestyles of their owners, were subject to minute restrictions and qualifications according to the particular samurai's stipend (income in terms of rice), and the stipend depended on the samurai's rank and position. This applied to everyone, from the feudal lord on down to the lowest foot soldier.

High-ranking samurai might have an annual stipend of 1,000 *koku* of rice (1 *koku* equals 180 liters) or more, but the majority, whether direct vassals of the shogunate or those in the service of individual domains, had stipends of some 100 to 500 *koku*. The houses of these lower-ranking samurai usually had a floor space of from 30 to 80 *tsubo* (1 *tsubo* equals 3.3 square meters), and everything from the construction of the gateway and the width of the vestibule to the type of circumferential rails and the decorative bordering of the *tatami* matting was strictly prescribed.

The arrangement of the rooms, while differing to a certain extent depending on the size of the house, was alike in the clear division between the section housing reception rooms for formal entertaining and the section intended for everyday living. In some cases, these sections were housed under separate roofs. The entrances too were divided into formal, kitchen, and rear entrances. Other common features were that earthen-floored spaces were small compared with those in farmhouses, and boarded floors were confined to the kitchen; most of the rest was *tatami*-floored.

In the feudal domains, samurai residences were often almost indistinguishable in size and style from those of the ordinary farmer.

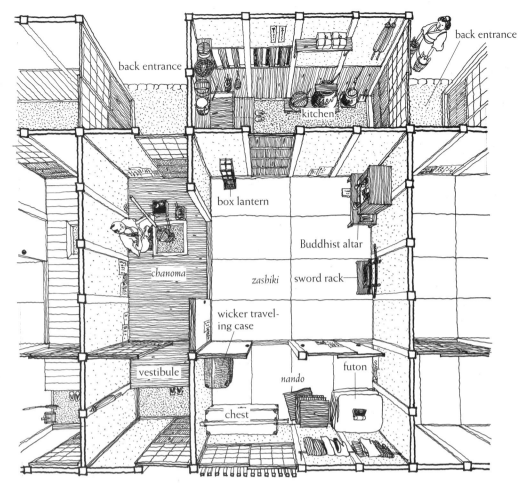

back entrance

back entrance

kitchen

box lantern

Buddhist altar

chanoma

zashiki

sword rack

wicker travel-
ing case

vestibule

futon

nando

chest

■ A Foot Soldier's Rowhouse

Samurai Rowhouses

In the mansions of feudal lords and other high-ranking warriors, whether located in Edo or in home domains, lower-ranking samurai and servants lived in rowhouses on the periphery of the compound. These rowhouses were partly defensive in nature, but they also served as status symbols, displaying for all to see the number of retainers that the lord had in his service. They were constructed in various sizes and styles, depending on the roles and ranks of the retainers who inhabited them. Most, however, had latticed windows with earthen walls that were wainscoted with wooden siding or tile and plaster.

Among these rowhouse was one of an unusual type known as a rowhouse gate (*nagaya-mon*). It consisted of a rowhouse with a built-in gate and guardhouse. It was permitted, at least in theory, only to those with stipends of 300 *koku* or more.

Some of the rowhouses of lower-ranking samurai, such as *ginmiyaku* (investigators), *ōnando* (stewards), and *ashigaru* (foot soldiers), were not within the mansion grounds. They were rather situated far from the mansion or castle, nearer the merchant quarter. Unlike the back-alley rowhouse of the ordinary townsfolk, however, each had its own gateway, if only a wooden gate in a fence. Each household had only two or three rooms of six or eight mats each, plus a kitchen, but even here detailed regulations stipulated the arrangement of rooms and their furnishing according to rank. Moreover, the distinction between reception room and the room, or rooms, for ordinary living was observed, and there were separate front and "kitchen" entrances.

A Variety of Towns

Post Towns

The *sankin-kōtai* system of alternate residence called for provincial lords to travel biannually between their territories and Edo. To provide places for the lord and his party to stay and to get a fresh supply of horses, post towns (*shukuba-machi*) were established on the five main highways leading from Edo and on other subsidiary highways.

Fifty-three such stations were officially established on the Tōkaidō highway, and sixty-seven on the Naka-Sendō. Each was provided with the following: agents to supply horses and ancillary manpower; official inns (*honjin*) and subsidiary inns (*waki-honjin*), where lords, samurai, and entourages could stay or rest up; and inns and tea-houses for ordinary travelers. The focal point of the post town was the *honjin*, which boasted reception rooms in the *shoin* style, living quarters in the townhouse style, and a gateway and garden of its own. At the entrances and exits to the town, courtyards with stone-paved or earthen embankments were built at right-angle bends in the road in order to slow any sudden influx of elements hostile to the shogunate.

With the establishment of a marketplace, a local commodities economy came into being, and in some cases a full-fledged town grew up, with a large number of merchants among its inhabitants.

Temple Towns

From the middle ages onward, large numbers of Shinto or Buddhist priests came to take up residence in the area "before the gateway" (*monzen*) of large Shinto shrines or Buddhist temples, with the result that markets sprang up and a "before-the-gate town" (*monzen-machi*) developed. Inns for people making pilgrimages to the shrine or temple, and shops catering to them, came to line the streets. Typical examples of such towns are Uji-Yamada (now Ise city) near the Grand Shrines of Ise, Sakamoto (now part of Ōtsu city) near Enryakuji temple, and Nara,

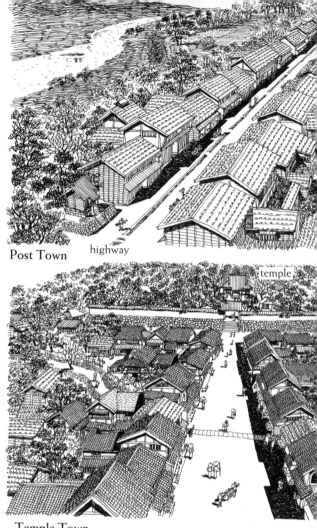

Post Town   highway

Temple Town

the site of Kōfukuji temple. Kotohira, Narita, and Zenkōji also flourished owing to the large numbers of sightseers they attracted. Even within existing cities such as Edo and Osaka, certain areas flourished because of the close proximity of temples or shrines and are thus considered *monzen-machi*.

Harbor Towns

Development of the great highways in the Edo period was paralleled by the development of sea transport, and harbor towns (*minato-machi*) prospered as receiving and distribution centers for various goods. Transport by sea—mainly of rice tribute and local specialty products—centered on two routes: the eastern route, from towns on the Japan Sea coast via the Tsugaru Straits to Edo; and the western route, from the Japan Sea coast to Osaka via Shimonoseki and

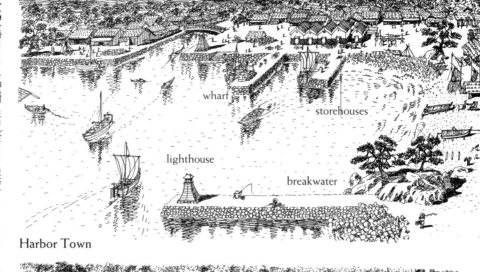

Harbor Town

Fishing Town

the Inland Sea. Leading port cities included Osaka, Edo, Tsuruga, Ōtsu, and Nagasaki.

It was in Osaka, however, the center of the nation's commerce and finance, that the main warehouse complexes grew up to provide domain storage, arrange sale of tribute, and sell local specialty products on behalf of the shogunate, feudal lords, and shogunate vassals, in addition to acting as trading centers. The merchants who conducted these activities lived in splendid mansions built in the fireproof storehouse (*dozō*) style (see p. 77) that had become common as a symbol of the wealthy merchant in Edo and other castle towns.

Fishing Towns

Traditionally most fishermen lived in villages where they engaged in a combination of small-scale fishing and farming. With the development of a monetary economy, however, individuals emerged who had amassed enough capital to engage in fishing on a grander scale, employing a large number of vessels and fishermen. Known as "net managers" (*amimoto*) or "boat owners" (*funanushi*), they came to control the ordinary fishermen in both financial and organizational terms.

Merchants and skilled workers dealing in fish and shellfish began to gather in places where the "net managers" were based, and inns and other facilities sprang up to meet their needs. The fishing towns (*ryōshi-machi*) that were the result differed from place to place, but boat houses and net sheds were generally located near the shore, with the ordinary fishermen living nearby. The house of the "net manager" was situated nearer the center of town, where it was safe in the event of a tidal wave.

■ Carpenters at Work

The labels in the illustration read: ripsaw, adze, elevation drawing, hammers, bench plane, measuring stick

Builders and Master Carpenters

Early in the Edo period, master carpenters (*tōryō*) were officially organized to undertake the building of castles and castle towns. They carried on the technical traditions learned in the Medieval period and attempted to reorganize themselves under the new regime of the Tokugawa shogunate and the feudal lords. Around the middle of the period, as the commodities economy became active in Edo, Osaka, Kyoto, and other large cities, the master carpenters banded together in guilds (*nakama*) to protect their mutual interests.

In the agricultural areas around the same time, there were farmers who did occasional work as carpenters or plasterers as time permitted. Some of these men eventually became full-time artisans, forming an independent class of specialists. As the commodities economy spread, an increasing number of these men moved to the cities, resulting in an expansion of the craftsmen class and creating a new breed of master carpenter. From this period on, construction work came to be conducted through a system of estimates and bidding.

Among the factors accounting for the spread of technology beyond the carpentry guilds were the development of proportional standards for structural parts to achieve overall architectural harmony; the publication of technical manuals; and the progressive availability on the market of boards, tiles, and other building materials. Other factors, too, contributed to the increased richness and variety of dwellings in the Edo period, such as the spread in the use of the ripsaw, which made the production of boards easier, and the reduction of time and trouble in the smoothing and leveling of wood thanks to use of the bench plane.

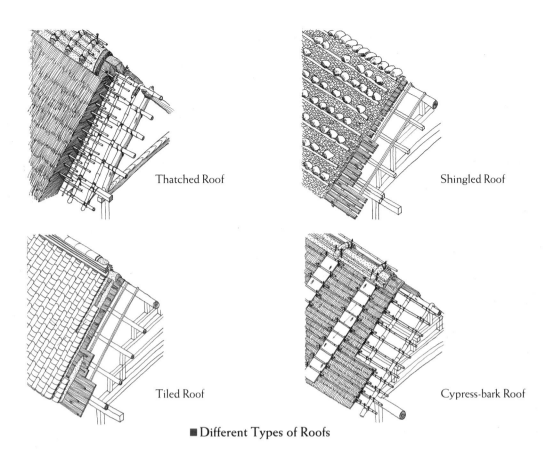

Thatched Roof

Shingled Roof

Tiled Roof

Cypress-bark Roof

■ Different Types of Roofs

Roof Types

Roofing material in the Edo period became richer in variety, and individual localities began to display characteristic styles of thatching and construction.

Materials used for covering roofs included reeds (*kaya*), wheat straw (*mugiwara*), rice straw (*inawara*), cypress bark (*hiwada*), cryptomeria bark (*sugikawa*), shingles, *hongawara-buki* (overlapping flat and rounded tiles), pantiles (*sangawara*), copper sheet, and slate. Slope, thatch foundation, and truss structure were largely determined by the type of roofing used.

Thatched Roofs

Thatching (*kayabuki*) commonly makes use of *susuki* (a variety of miscanthus grass) or *yoshi* (also called *ashi*; ditch reed), though it may be mixed with wheat straw. The slope of the roof is at least 45 degrees, and much steeper in districts with heavy snowfall. Usually the thatch is placed with the root ends pointing downward, although in some districts the reverse is found.

Shingled Roofs

The overall term *ita-buki* (shingling) covers two types: *kokera-buki*, where small, thin boards of cryptomeria, cypress, or other wood are overlapped and weighted down with wood or rocks, and *tochi-buki*, where longer, thicker shingles are used.

Tiled Roofs

Tiling was the rule in samurai residences, but in Kyoto-Osaka and other districts to the west tile was used on the houses of the common people as well. In Edo, pantiles were invented around the middle of the Edo period and came into general use on account of their resistance to fire, typhoons, and other forces of nature.

Cryptomeria-bark Roofs

Afforestation of cryptomeria trees began in the Edo period, and roofs covered with their bark became common in mountainous areas, along with thatched roofs. This had the advantage of cheapness, since the bark from trees felled for their timber could be used. Cypress bark, however, was considered to be superior.

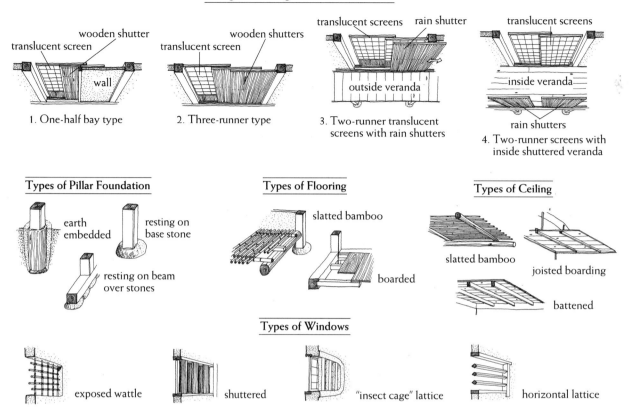

Changes in Sliding Screens and Shutters

1. One-half bay type

translucent screen
wooden shutter
wall

2. Three-runner type

translucent screen
wooden shutters

3. Two-runner translucent screens with rain shutters

translucent screens
rain shutter
outside veranda

4. Two-runner screens with inside shuttered veranda

translucent screens
inside veranda
rain shutters

Types of Pillar Foundation

earth embedded
resting on base stone
resting on beam over stones

Types of Flooring

slatted bamboo
boarded

Types of Ceiling

slatted bamboo
joisted boarding
battened

Types of Windows

exposed wattle
shuttered
"insect cage" lattice
horizontal lattice

Sophisticated Techniques

The dwellings of the Edo period showed remarkable advances in building technique, and wooden architecture reached a high degree of technical sophistication.

Pillars usually rested on base stones, which were set in firmly compacted earth. The bases of the pillars were carved to fit the shape of the stone. Horizontal beams resting on base stones (groundsills) were used in storehouses, stables, and other structures where the base of the pillars was liable to damage.

Sliding screens and other partitions, combined with verandas, were modified so as to obviate the restrictive feeling of solid walls and to provide more sunlight and air. The arrangement of wooden shutters and translucent screens, which at first permitted a width of only half a bay in terms of light or open space, gave way to a three-runner arrangement. Then, with the addition of a box for holding the wooden shutters, wooden shutters became "rain shutters" (*amado*) for use at

night and as protection against rainfall. Consequently, the whole space between pillars could be opened at will. Along with this, the hitherto external veranda was brought inside, thus coming to form an integral part of the interior space.

In farmhouses, older types of flooring such as slatted bamboo were replaced almost entirely by wooden floors as the emergence of professional sawyers using the ripsaw led to plentiful supplies of boards.

Ceilings changed, too. As various types and sizes of movable braziers came into use for heating apart from the traditional sunken fireplace, the slatted bamboo ceiling, which had permitted smoke and steam to escape freely, came to be replaced in areas for formal use by joisted or battened ceilings.

All kinds of windows, too, were devised, not just to provide light and air, but to give variety to the exterior of the building. Even so, official prohibitions and restrictions on extravagance kept them, generally speaking, within the bounds dictated by the owner's social status.

The Modern Period

Meiji Period
(1868–1912)

Taishō Period
(1912–1926)

Shōwa Period
(1926-89)

Heisei Period
(1989–present)

In 1868 the Tokugawa government collapsed, ushering in a new era of modern government. Emperor Meiji left Kyoto and took up residence in Edo, which was renamed Tokyo ("Eastern Capital") and became the capital of the nation. This era of transition is called the Meiji Restoration (referring to the "restoration" of the emperor as the rightful head of state instead of the shogun), and the reign of Emperor Meiji is known as the Meiji period.

The shogunate had lasted for over two and a half centuries, being gradually undermined by factors both internal and external. At home, the development of a commodity economy had created inner tensions; abroad, demands for the opening of the country had come to exert irresistible pressure on the shogunate's policy of enforced seclusion; and finally, in 1858, the conclusion of the U.S.-Japanese Treaty of Amity and Commerce led to the opening of the country, followed by the collapse of the shogunate and the establishment of a constitutional monarchy.

The Meiji period was characterized by a rejection of the systems and culture of the Edo period and the promotion of capitalist development and modernization—here, virtually synonymous with Westernization. The government introduced modern industries and pressed ahead with industrialization in order to achieve equality with the advanced nations of the West. Industrial capitalists emerged to replace the commercial capitalists of the past, and new working and middle classes came into being that were to prove the driving force of the new era.

New government buildings were erected in the Western style as symbols of a modern society, and politicians began to live in Western-style homes. Railways were built, and horse trams and rickshaws began to ply the streets, which were transformed by rows of brick buildings and gas lamps. Modern factories went up all over the country. Workers were recruited to work in them, and university graduates from the middle class were trained to supervise and run them.

With its successes in the Sino-Japanese (1894-95) and Russo-Japanese (1904-05) wars, Japan emerged as a military power to be reckoned with. It used the might of its industrial capital to gain control of Korea and Formosa (Taiwan), then embarked on aggression in China and eventually, in the name of the "Greater East Asia Co-Prosperity Sphere," sent forces into Southeast Asia and finally launched the Pacific War.

It was during the Meiji period that Japanese houses underwent their first great changes. The nature of those changes was foretold in a novel published in 1909 by Natsume Sōseki, *After That* (*Sore Kara*). Sōseki wrote, "Modern Society, as Daisuke saw things, was no more than an assemblage of isolated individuals; land itself had a natural continuity, but once houses were built on it, it was immediately split into pieces, and the people who lived in the houses were similarly split up into individuals. Modern civilization isolated us all...."

Concerning middle-class homes in Tokyo, Sōseki's hero says: "In the extreme shoddiness and ugliness of its construction—so it seemed to Daisuke in particular—Hiraoka's house fully demonstrated the progressive impoverishment of the middle class occasioned by the rise in prices of the past dozen years or so. A mere two yards separated the gateway and front entrance. It was the same with the back entrance, and similar mean dwellings stood both behind the house and to both sides. They were tokens of the struggle for survival, set up with as little expense as possible by capitalists of the lowest order, tempted by the prospect of twenty or thirty percent profit on their paltry outlays to take advantage of the squalid expansion of the city of Tokyo. Tokyo by now, particularly its poorer quarters, was dotted all over with houses of this kind. What was more, they were increasing at an extraordinary rate, like fleas brought forth by the rainy season. Daisuke had once labeled them the 'development of despair,' and

he considered them to be the most appropriate symbol of present-day Japan."

This passage, though written over ninety years ago, was to prove relevant in the years to come and even to some extent today.

The Meiji Restoration and Western-style Architecture

Determined to strengthen the country and achieve parity with the advanced capitalist nations of the West, the new Meiji government set about laying the foundations of a wealthy and militarily powerful nation by establishing a constitutional monarchy and encouraging the growth of capitalism. It began by bringing in modern Western technology and establishing modern industries.

In 1870 the government set up a Ministry of Industrial Works (Kōbushō) to promote industrial development. It placed mines, iron manufacture, shipbuilding, railways, and communications under government management, and set about promoting these government-run industries by building machinery and chemical factories and establishing model silk and cotton-spinning mills. It also established an Engineering College (Kōbu Daigakkō) in order to train government officials as technical experts. At the same time, a large number of Western experts were brought in to teach the relevant technology.

Many such experts, as well as Western merchants, diplomats, and others, took up residence in foreign concessions created in port cities such as Nagasaki, Kobe, and Yokohama. This fact led to the building of many Western-style homes and commercial buildings (*ijin-kan*) to house these foreigners and their businesses. Their lifestyles differed radically from those of the Japanese. The houses with their Western-style verandas and shutters, the chairs and tables, the fireplaces, Western dress (including shoes and hats), food and drink (including beef, wine, and whisky)—all were astonishing to any Japanese who saw them.

The new capital of Tokyo (formerly Edo) also

■ The Ginza in the Early Meiji Period

began to develop a Western facade. The Hibiya and Nagata-chō area, once the site of the residences of feudal lords, became a center of government ministries and agencies. The streets, improved and reorganized, were soon busily plied by rickshaws and horse-drawn carriages. In 1872 a railway was opened between Yokohama and Shinbashi in central Tokyo. The main street of the Ginza district saw the rise of two-story brick buildings, and gas street lamps also appeared. Eventually there were even buses and streetcars drawn by horses.

A phrase often used in connection with Westernization in the Meiji period was *wakon yōsai* ("the Japanese spirit with Western technology"). In short, the priority was the introduction of modern Western technology; understanding the underlying culture and profiting from it spiritually was left to a later date. Even so, the process

of learning from large numbers of foreign technical experts inevitably brought some knowledge of the history, culture, and social systems of their homelands. The number of Japanese who went abroad to study gradually grew, producing an increasing understanding of Western society.

During the first stage of architectural activity in the Meiji period, Western-style government offices and other institutions under official purview (such as school buildings) were designed by foreign architects. In the second stage, these same architects designed residences for government officials and the upper class of society. In the final stage, native Japanese architects began to participate in building privately owned companies, factories, warehouses, and residences.

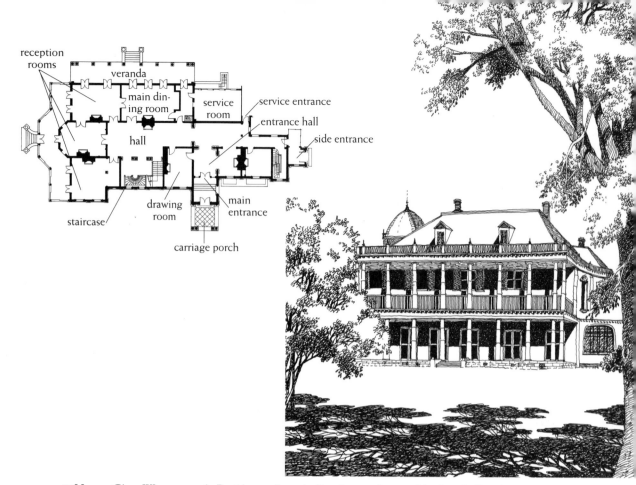

reception rooms

veranda

main dining room

service room

service entrance

entrance hall

side entrance

hall

drawing room

main entrance

staircase

carriage porch

■ Upper-Class Western-style Residence: Iwasaki Residence, designed by Josiah Condor, 1891

Western-style Residences

Even before the fall of the Tokugawa shogunate, Western-style residences had existed for the use of foreign diplomats and merchants. It was not until Western food, clothing, and other foreign ways had been partially assimilated in the last decade of the nineteenth century, however, that Japanese began building them for their own use. Even then, residences in the Western style were limited to a very small segment of society, mostly the nobility, high-ranking government officials, and the *zaibatsu* business conglomerates. Such undertakings were prohibitively expensive: building materials such as brick, iron, and glass had to be imported, and foreign experts had to be employed to design and supervise the work. From around 1890, when the first graduates of the Engineering College began working as architects and the initial rush of pro-

jects for the government was over, Japanese architects were able to work for private capital as well, and from then on much of their work was commissioned by industrial capitalists.

The Western "residences" built in this way were not so much residences as wings devoted to the entertainment of distinguished guests. The owner and his family lived in Japanese-style homes connected to this wing by a common vestibule or a corridor. Their Japanese home was, in essence, a simplified form of the *shoin* style, divided into formal and family sections. The formal section consisted chiefly of the head of the household's quarters and a room, or rooms, used for casual entertaining, with a *zashiki* containing a decorative alcove and staggered shelves.

Thus Western-style residential structures of the day were subsidiary structures, built chiefly as symbols of social status.

Drawing Room of the
Niijima Residence, 1878

Kitchen of the Iwasaki
Residence, 1891

■ Interior of Western-style Residences

Western-style Dwellings and Daily Life

The adoption of Western-style clothing and food was relatively rapid, but the use of tables and chairs and the lifestyle they implied did not begin to make headway until around 1890. It must be remembered that the traditional Japanese manner was to squat or sit on *tatami* mats, making use of full-sized tables and chairs only on special occasions, if ever. Similarly, greetings were conducted from a kneeling or sitting position.

As early as 1871 it had become a matter of policy that government offices should make use of chairs and tables and that greetings should be exchanged with both parties standing. However, these practices were confined to government agencies, schools, and the military. In everyday life, the custom of doing everything seated on *tatami* remained intact. A generalized Western lifestyle did not spread until gas or electric lighting, water mains, gas heating, and Western-style furniture came into common use.

In high society, people were obliged to live a kind of double life. Their ordinary life was carried out in a *tatami*-floored Japanese wing while the entertaining of guests was done in the Western wing, with everything from drawing rooms to recreational rooms being in the "table-and-chairs" style.

The kitchen was one of the last parts of the house to be Westernized. In a few upper-class Western-style residences, kitchen equipment was imported from abroad and the cooks worked while standing, but in most kitchens the traditional arrangement persisted in which there was a floor-level sink in an earthen-floored or boarded area. It was not until around the first decade of the twentieth century that the floor-level sink finally gave way to the sink at which one worked standing.

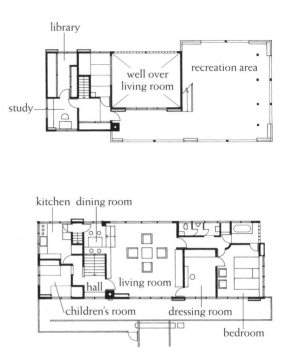

■ Modern Home Built in Early Shōwa Period: Wakasa Residence, designed by Horiguchi Sutemi, 1931

The Modernization of Housing

Following the Sino-Japanese (1894-95) and Russo-Japanese (1904-05) wars, the Meiji government pursued increasingly aggressive policies toward continental China and the Korean peninsula, working hand in hand with the *zaibatsu* business conglomerates. At the same time, the *zaibatsu* stepped up the concentration and monopolization of wealth, giving society an increasingly capitalist flavor. Partly in reaction to this, the Taishō period (1912–26) saw the emergence of workers' and farmers' movements, and a general climate evolved that favored democratic reform, as summed up in the phrase "Taishō democracy."

Within the construction world, which until then had been preoccupied with introducing and absorbing Western architectural technology so as to create a solid grounding of modern professional skills, a movement arose calling for the development of better houses and the improvement of everyday life. The Japanese dwelling

thus far, even where it was influenced by Western architecture, was essentially premodern. Its eye was directed chiefly to entertaining, with the head of the family at its center, and the forms of the feudal home continued largely unchanged. From here on, however, the emphasis gradually began to shift to family life.

It was largely due to the climate created in the Taishō era, under the influence of the Secessionist movement in post–World War I Europe, that the first native architectural movement, the Bunriha (Secessionist Faction), was born in 1920. Its underlying philosophy called for a new form of architectural expression suited to modern industrial society. This would include, in housing as elsewhere, the creation of bold spatial compositions combining lines and surfaces, together with functional planning of areas and the use for expressive purposes of reinforced concrete, steel frames, and dry construction. The houses that were actually designed, however, were confined to a very small number of upper-class residences or to the architects' own homes.

■ Living and Dining Rooms: Wakasa Residence

New Dwellings in the Towns

With the rapid increase in urban population that accompanied the development of a capitalist society after World War I, the problem of creating proper housing for urban workers drew increasing attention. Until then, most urban workers had to be satisfied with cramped, rented homes in rundown parts of the traditionally plebeian areas of the city. As the number of middle-class office workers increased, they began to want better living conditions and homes of their own. They were getting used to Western-style living habits, and they were no longer satisfied with Japanese-style rented houses. Thus the model housing displays that began to be held in Tokyo and Osaka in the early 1920s evoked a warm response. The development of new residential areas by privately owned railway companies, which had lines running out into the suburbs, further fanned the desire for

a home of one's own. *Bunka jūtaku* ("culture houses") began to appear in large numbers in high-class residential areas and on the outskirts of the cities. They were structurally Japanese but incorporated a Western drawing room and other non-Japanese elements (see p. 102).

Around the same time, young Japanese architects influenced by modern international movements grew dissatisfied with hybrid Japanese-Western houses and began to seek something more modern and family oriented. Such ideas were given practical expression in the houses they designed for the upper classes and for themselves (see illustration above). Increasingly, the homes of the middle class and above came to place more emphasis on the daily life of the family than on entertaining: living and dining rooms in the Western style became the focus of the home and privacy was provided by the incorporation of individual bedrooms and children's rooms.

The Inequalities of Modernization

Modernization and Westernization did not, unfortunately, improve the lot of all citizens equally. The regime established by the Meiji government—composed of the military, the bureaucracy, the privileged capitalist class, and the landowners, all focusing on the emperor system—weighed heavily on the general population. The lot of miners and small farmers was especially hard.

In theory, modern society had abolished almost all class distinctions, but in practice the people had merely been reorganized into two great divisions: on the one hand, the privileged consisting of the imperial family, the nobility, and the ex-samurai class, and on the other the common people. The new class rankings that came with the development of capitalism only served to aggravate social discrimination.

In its initial stages the promotion of industry as part of the modernization and Westernization of the country proceeded under state management, and was largely backed by agricultural taxes and the income from raw silk and tea, which at the time accounted for sixty percent of all exports.

In 1873 the land tax system was revised, private ownership of land was recognized, and restrictions on buying and selling land were removed. Henceforth, instead of rendering tribute as in the Edo period, farmers paid a tax on the value of their land. Although this tax was a seemingly light three percent, it amounted to the equivalent of some thirty percent of the value of their crops. As a result, many farmers were obliged to sell their land and become tenants, giving rise, in consequence, to a class of powerful landowners. Moreover, as the rent of the tenant farmers proved insupportable, many of them gave up agriculture altogether and became factory workers or coal miners. The labor needed by modern industry was largely supplied by this floating population of onetime farmers, who tended to concentrate in the towns

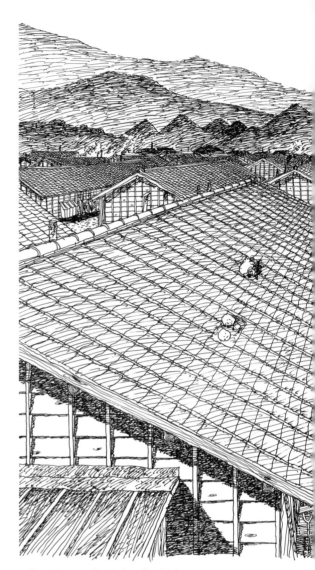

■ Rowhouses Built for Coal Miners

where the factories were. This was the backdrop against which the progress of modernization in the nation's urban centers took place.

The mining of silver, copper, and coal constituted one of the most profitable government-run industries, and much of the labor force for these mines was provided by farmers and other people at the bottom of the social scale, who worked under the harshest conditions.

Coal mines played a particularly important role in industrialization, as shown by their already being in operation at the end of the Edo period as part of domanial efforts to promote industry. Once they were placed under government management as a source of energy for modern indus-

try, foreign mining experts were brought in and modern technology introduced. In spite of this technological innovation in the coal mines, laborers were no better off than in other mines, and the makeup of the labor force was essentially the same. In time it became so difficult to recruit new miners that convicts were conscripted. By around the middle of the Meiji period, convicts accounted for fifty to seventy percent of all coal miners.

At the Miike and Takashima mines in Kyū-shū, supervision of miners was left in the hands of subcontractors. These subcontractors housed workers under the most degraded conditions, kept them under continual surveillance, used force to maintain control, and then skimmed off a portion of their pay. The miners lived in row-houses in groups of four to one four-mat room. These rooms were not provided with a door or sliding screen at the entrance so that their every move might be constantly observed. Married people were housed, two couples each, in rooms of four to six mats, with no facilities save a sink and cooking stove. Even in the back-street rowhouses of the Edo period, conditions had not been as bad. Thus, while "modernization" resulted in the adoption of some of the more showy aspects of Western civilization, beneath the surface it often created working and living conditions of the severest sort.

The "Inner Corridor" Type House

A new type of house plan came into being near the end of the Meiji period and at the beginning of the Taishō period, the interior-corridor house (*nakarōka-shiki jūtaku*). Nearly eighty percent of urban workers in the Meiji period lived in rented houses, of which approximately half measured 15 mats or less in floor space—that is, two six-mat rooms and one three-mat room (one mat eguals approximately 174 by 87 cm.). However, the more affluent middle class wanted something more, and that need was met by the inner-corridor house. A hybrid construction grafting a Western-style drawing room onto a basically Japanese home, its rooms were arranged to the north and south of a central corridor. First appearing in the early to middle 1910s, it served as the typical middle-class dwelling from then on and through the Shōwa period (1926–89).

Although this type of house was created under Western influence in that it used a central corridor to give a certain amount of independence to individual rooms, the only purely Western element was the drawing-room–cum–study, which was situated to one side of the vestibule; the other rooms were in the Japanese style.

The central corridor ran from east to west. The family's living quarters lay to the south of it, with a veranda attached. These quarters consisted of an eight- to ten-mat formal *zashiki* with a decorative alcove and staggered shelves, an anteroom, a living room, and a sitting room. On the north side there was a toilet situated near the vestibule, a kitchen, a bathroom, a back entrance, and, invariably, a maid's room. Reasonable though this arrangement may seem, there was still little privacy—the rooms being divided up by paper- or cloth-covered sliding screens—while the general atmosphere, with its emphasis on entertaining and the head of the family, was still premodern.

■ Layout of a Typical "Inner Corridor" Type Residence

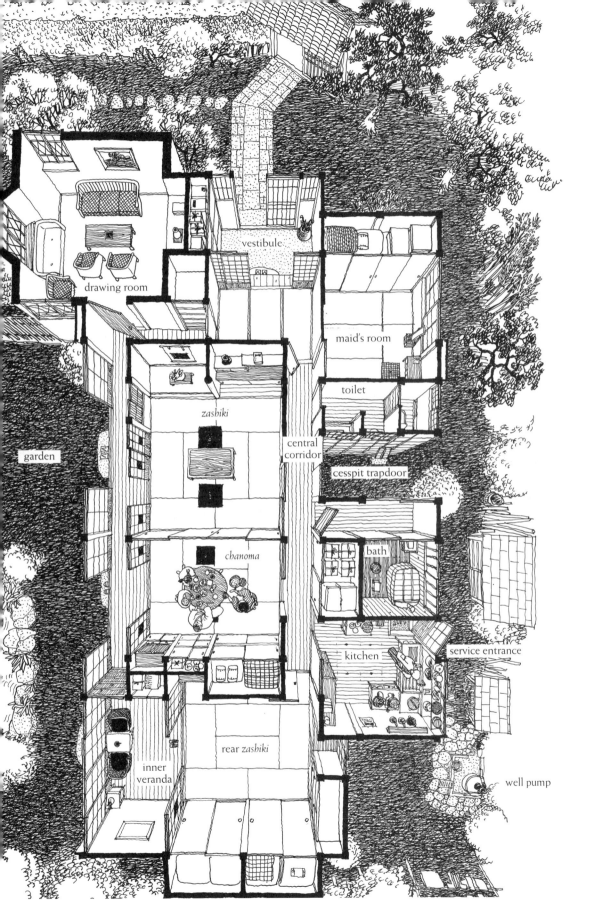

drawing room

vestibule

garden

maid's room

toilet

zashiki

central corridor

cesspit trapdoor

chanoma

bath

service entrance

kitchen

rear *zashiki*

inner veranda

well pump

■ Two-story Rowhouse of Around 1930

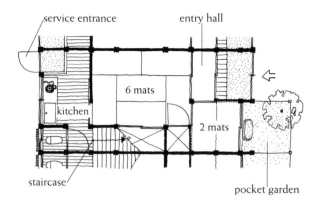

service entrance   entry hall

6 mats

kitchen

2 mats

staircase

pocket garden

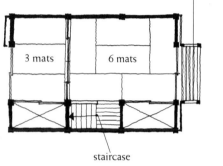

laundry balcony

3 mats   6 mats

staircase

Modern Rowhouses

The rowhouse (*nagaya*), which had been the typical dwelling of the common people since the Edo period, continued to serve the same role throughout the Meiji period and beyond, undergoing certain changes in form.

Even at the end of the Edo period, the overcrowded urban areas assigned to the plebeian classes had already begun to sprawl, but this tendency was intensified in the Meiji era as rowhouses were thrown up in flourishing industrial districts to accommodate coal heavers, stevedores, and other laborers. Increasingly crowded, such residential areas occasionally turned into disfiguring slums dotted with numerous flophouses.

Although not as bad as the coal miners', these rowhouses had ten to twenty units under one roof, were constructed on poorly drained ground on confined lots, and shared unsanitary communal wells and privies. These disgraceful conditions finally began to show improvement from 1907 onward, when structural restrictions were imposed on rowhouses and the slums began to be cleared. Even in the mid-1910s, at the beginning of the Taishō period (1912–26), however, one-third of housing in the large cities was of the rowhouse type.

In the 1910s, two-story rowhouses began to appear, the number of rooms increased, and private toilets began to be installed. On the other hand, structural overcrowding deprived inhabitants of sunlight.

In the aftermath of the Great Kantō Earthquake of 1923, Tokyo rowhouses took a turn for the better. Homes with greater independence—only two to four units under one roof—were built, each with a pocket garden next to the entrance (see illustration at left). With the spread of public water, drains, and gas, the kitchen came to be placed at the rear of the unit, not near the entrance facing the alleyway as was customary.

■ A Dōjunkai Apartment and the Communal Laundry Area on the Roof

Apartments

The first apartment buildings to be constructed in Tokyo as a new form of housing for the masses went up around the end of the Meiji era, in the first decade of the twentieth century. Since the rent was high, they ended up being inhabited only by special people, such as novelists and artists freshly back from Europe, which was the original home of the apartment house. Among ordinary people, they did not come into use until after the Great Kantō Earthquake of 1923.

From 1926 until 1934 the Dōjunkai, an association set up in 1924 for the relief of quake victims, built a series of reinforced-concrete apartment houses for working people. They contained two types of units of various sizes and arrangements: those for single people and for families. A number of experimental features were introduced: elevators, kitchens with dust chutes, communal baths, barbershops, and communal areas for washing and drying clothes on the rooftop. Tenants were restricted to "working people," but in practice most were middle-class and apparently the object of considerable envy among row-house dwellers.

The number of these apartments built was not large, but their form had a good deal of influence on ordinary people's dwellings, and private firms began to construct more and more Dōjunkai-type apartment houses. On the other hand, many shoddy wooden apartment houses were also built, producing poor living conditions. Even so, the Dōjunkai apartment houses had provided ample food for thought concerning housing in overcrowded cities, and their example was still referred to in post–World War II Japan.

■ Kitchen of Working Class Home in the City

■ Examples of Children's Room and Bedroom Proposed as Part of Housing Improvement Movement

Modernization of the House in the Taishō Period

Although the modernization of the house had been under way since the beginning of the Meiji era, it consisted at first of little more than an imitation of Western lifestyles. Then, as chairs and tables began to be used in companies, government offices, schools, and hospitals, and people gradually got used to life using gas, water mains, and electric lighting, modernization went ahead more positively, evolving new forms such as the central-corridor type discussed above.

Against a background of progressively avail-able public facilities, the Taishō period (1912–26) saw new moves to improve housing and reform lifestyles. The move to modernize housing was reflected mainly in the dwellings of the middle and upper classes in large cities, where it gave birth to the "culture house" (*bunka jūtaku*; see p. 99). Houses of this type, however, were still not generally available. The contrast between the reality and the ideal can be seen in the illustrations above, even though the kitchen at the top shows many improvements, such as the standup sink, gas stove, and ice box. It was not until after the end of World War II that genuine modernization took place.

Postwar Housing—Rebuilding Amidst the Rubble

On August 15, 1945, Japan surrendered unconditionally to the Allied powers, bringing the Pacific War to an end. This event marked the collapse of the governmental system that had been in effect since the early days of the Meiji period, which was centered ultimately on the emperor and promoted policies of national wealth, military might, and industrial expansion.

As a result of the war, 160 cities throughout the nation had been at least fifty percent destroyed, and 2.1 million houses had been razed by fire, while another 550,000 had been demolished to create firebreaks. Adding to the shortage of 1.18 million houses that had already existed during the war, the demand for housing from the postwar influx of repatriates from the continent brought the total shortage up to around 4.2 million.

Even before the end of the war, the nation had been plagued by inflation, the result of the steady expansion of the military supply industries since war broke out between Japan and China in 1937. The housing situation was particularly bad for workers in the cities; due to shortages of building materials and labor, they had to be content with the inferior structures known as "national housing." The scale of the houses provided by the Housing Corporation (Jūtaku Eidan) set up in 1941 grew gradually smaller, till toward the end of the war tiny houses covering a mere 21 square meters were being built. In other cases, an existing house designed for one family was split up to accommodate two or more. In theory, such "homes" were planned so as to keep eating and sleeping areas separate, but in fact they were little better than places to bed down for the night.

Long accustomed to the austerities of the war years, the nation was awakened as from a nightmare by the end of hostilities. People began immediately to salvage from the rubble anything that could be used to make a shelter. Those who

■ Makeshift Dwellings in the Aftermath of World War II

could make a crude hut from charred timbers or mangled tin sheets were lucky; many had to make do with a gutted bus or what remained of an air-raid shelter.

This terrible experience gave some people second thoughts about the housing of the past. How could minimal building materials be used to best advantage? How could one put a minimum of space to the best use? Had not the prewar home attached too much weight to

entertaining visitors and shown insufficient concern for the housewife...?

In November of the year the war ended, a governmental agency for the reconstruction of devastated cities (Sensai Fukkō-in) was established and plans made for the provision of housing, but its activities were severely hampered by the extreme shortage of materials. Generally, it was forbidden to construct houses of more than 12 *tsubo* (1 *tsubo* equals 3.3 square meters). Houses for rent under prefectural control measured an average 6.5 *tsubo*. This figure was subsequently expanded to from 10 to 12 *tsubo*, but such restrictions did not finally disappear until 1950. During this period, various forward-looking housing proposals were made by architects, and deeply ingrained feudalistic ideas were at long last uprooted.

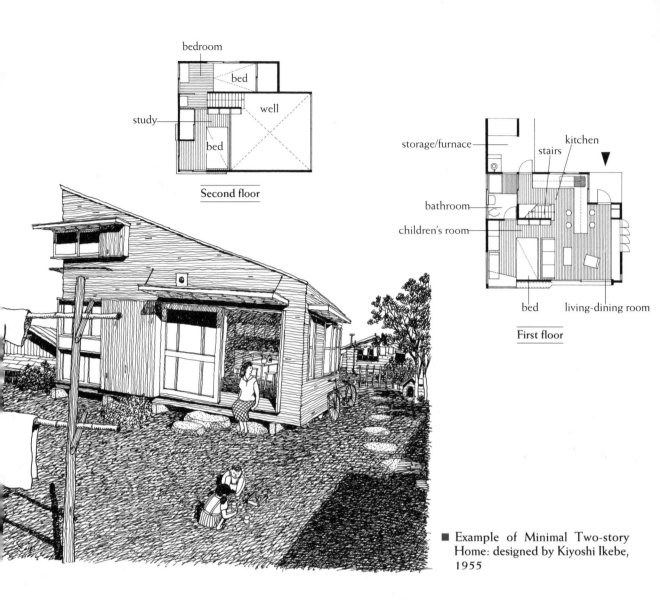

bedroom

bed

well

study

bed

Second floor

storage/furnace

kitchen

stairs

bathroom

children's room

bed   living-dining room

First floor

■ Example of Minimal Two-story Home: designed by Kiyoshi Ikebe, 1955

New Housing Proposals

Once the chaotic immediate postwar period was over, people finally shook off the mental shackles of militarism and began to look forward to a new, more democratic society. In 1947, a new constitution was enacted providing for the sovereignty of the people, the establishment of basic human rights, and the renunciation of war. In 1950 the outbreak of the Korean War led to a boom engendered by U.S. military procurement, and the Japanese economy, led by the iron and steel industry, enjoyed a sudden prosperity.

In 1950, as part of the government's housing policy, a Housing Loan Law (*jūtaku kin'yu kōko-hō*) was enacted as a means of promoting home ownership. Although those eligible to borrow funds needed to have some personal capital and a fixed income equivalent to seven times the mortgage payments, the law served to make the middle class aware of the advantages of home ownership.

Architects, newly invigorated by the tasks that lay before them, proposed such schemes as factory-produced homes aiming to reduce costs through mass production; tiny houses covering only six *tsubo*; low-cost housing; and minimal housing that still preserved privacy by the use of wells and mezzanine floors.

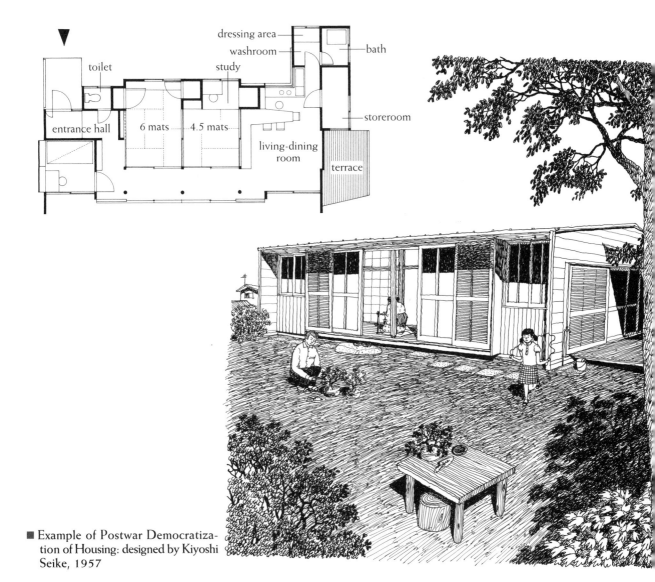

Example of Postwar Democratization of Housing: designed by Kiyoshi Seike, 1957

Plan labels: dressing area, washroom, bath, toilet, study, storeroom, entrance hall, 6 mats, 4.5 mats, living-dining room, terrace

A Variety of Experiments

The architectural experiments of the 1950s were all the more ambitious in that there was as yet no chance to build large, non-residential buildings. In main, they sought to keep the different functions of the home separate while creating a convincing spatial blend. A variety of techniques were explored, from wells and skip floors to pilotis and movable partitions for dividing up what was basically a single large room. Eventually the building of small detached dwellings in the city drove up land prices, which led in turn to the urbanization of neighboring agricultural communities.

The new type of house was generally centered on the family, with the living room and dining room as its twin focuses. These were the most social spaces, serving both as a gathering place for the family and as a place to receive guests. On the other hand, the husband and wife's bedroom and the children's room, or rooms, were the most personalized, separated by walls rather than by sliding screens and entered through lockable doors to ensure privacy. The kitchen was designed to lighten the housewife's burden, and importance was attached to its relationship, in terms of practical convenience, to the vestibule, bathroom, and toilet.

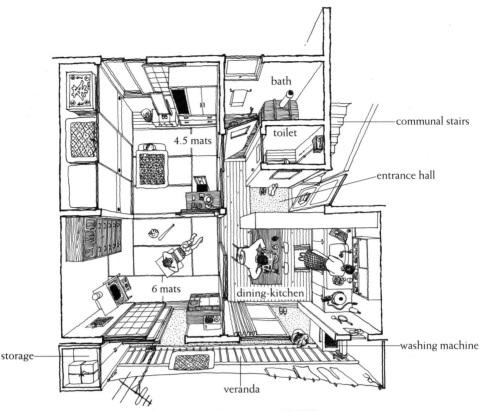

bath

communal stairs

4.5 mats

toilet

entrance hall

6 mats

dining-kitchen

storage

washing machine

veranda

■ Japan Housing Corporation Apartment, 2DK Type

Apartment House Complexes (*Danchi*)

Probably one of the most decisive events in the history of postwar housing was the government decision to provide rental apartments blocks (*danchi*) in large quantities for workers in the cities, in particular for ordinary people of the middle and working classes. The number of homes built in the first five years after the war was small, but from the time of the establishment of the Japan Housing Corporation (Nihon Jūtaku Kōdan) in 1955, the supply swelled in scale and number, creating a class of people known popularly as *danchi-zoku*, "*danchi*-dwellers."

The Corporation set about reducing the distance between workplace and home by making use of existing residential areas and erecting apartment buildings with stores and offices on the first floor and apartments from the second floor up, and by redeveloping certain areas to permit erection of high-rise apartment blocks. At the same time, on the outskirts of existing cities, it built "new towns,"

each containing several thousands of homes.

These Corporation apartment buildings ranged in height from four or five stories to more than a dozen stories. Their construction was accompanied by efforts to improve the environment through rezoning the land and providing facilities such as parks for children, parking areas, and bicycle lots.

The standard arrangement of rooms was "2DK" (two rooms with a dining-kitchen area), with 1DK apartments for single persons and 3DK and 4DK apartments for larger families. The Corporation was the first to build apartments with a combined dining room and kitchen. Each apartment also had its own bathroom. There was some criticism of the cramped space (the phrase "*danchi* size" came to be used to indicate a general scaling down of traditional specifications, such as those of *tatami* mats), but they were usually more spacious than the apartments ("mansions") being built by private firms, and they marked the beginning of a new age in their improvements in such facilities as the kitchen sink.

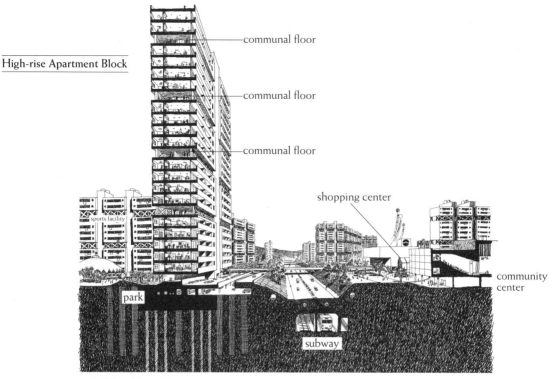

High-rise Apartment Block

communal floor

communal floor

communal floor

shopping center

sports facility

community center

park

subway

■ A "New Town"

High-Rise Housing and the New Towns

One means of making effective use of the limited land in urban areas has been increasing the number of high-rise apartment buildings. This was made possible in 1965 by the repeal of a 1920 law that restricted multistory buildings to a height of thirty-one meters. The principal driving force behind the construction of high-rise dwellings has been the high cost of land, the general shortage of housing, and the fact that open spaces can be easily created around such structures. One of the first to be built was in Kobe City, but it soon became apparent that high-rises entailed many unforeseen problems, such as the handling of garbage and mail, the distance between residences and children's play areas, and safety considerations in the event of fire or earthquake. In providing housing in the form of high-rise dwellings, it became clear that careful consideration must also be given to questions of transportation, supporting facilities, and the effects of the buildings on the surrounding neighborhood.

To some extent, the concept of the "new town" was intended to address these problems. Proposed in Great Britain in the 1940s, it called for the creation of towns that would relocate populations away from large cities by creating autonomous communities complete with homes, hospitals, businesses, schools, and shopping and cultural centers.

One of the best-known new towns in Japan is Tama New Town, located west of Tokyo. Planning began in 1963, construction in 1967, and occupancy in 1971. One feature of this town is the large number of high-rise multidwelling buildings, with their attendant problems. A number of other new towns have also been built, including those in Senri and Senboku near Osaka.

While these new towns were conceived as self-contained environments, they still have not met expectations in all areas of concern, such as livability, higher education, and transportation. Further, rather than being self-supporting areas in which inhabitants work locally, new towns tend to be appendages or "bed towns" of nearby metropolises, with many people commuting to work or school. Various problems remain to be worked out before new towns can be considered fully functional.

Housing Developments

Housing developments are a predominant sign of the urbanization of the countryside. The sites, carved out of what was agricultural or wooded land, often have many disadvantages, such as a lack of proper community facilities. Demand, however, remains high among people who dream of owing a home of their own.

Prefabricated Homes

Built by assembling factory-made sections, these houses aim to combine better quality with cheapness, but costs often remain high, while standardization makes them unadaptable to the varied needs of their inhabitants.

"Two-by-four" Homes

The "two-by-four" frame construction method, imported from the United States, involves the use of standardized lumber that is usually two inches thick and four inches wide. It has the advantage of cheapness and simplicity, but has yet to adapt itself fully to the Japanese scene.

Capsule Apartments

This method entails attaching mass-produced compartments, not unlike space capsules, to a basic framework. It has the advantages of saving time and reducing construction costs, but many problems remain concerning interchangeability and replaceability.

A New Housing Industry and Innovation in Residential Architecture

The boom sparked in 1950 by U.S. military procurement for the Korean War led to a remarkable revolution in technology under the aegis of the newly resurgent *zaibatsu* conglomerates. There was a great expansion in machinery and equipment and an increase in the number of factories. In the 1960s this resulted in a period of rapid economic growth, and toward the end of the decade, housing overtook automobile manufacturing as the leading Japanese industry.

The twin pillars of postwar housing policy were the encouragement of home ownership by the Housing Loan Corporation and the provision of homes by the Japan Housing Corporation, but their efforts proved insufficient to satisfy public demand, either quantitatively or qualitatively. Private firms, too, made an effort to improve quality and lower costs by mass-producing prefabricated parts in the same way that other industries did. However, with the increase in individual income that accompanied high economic growth, the demand for new homes spiraled. As a result, major trading, construction, railway, and shipbuilding companies turned to the housing industry as a new business opportunity.

To a certain extent, these companies were able to satisfy public demand with housing developments (*bunjō jūtaku*), prefabricated housing, and condominiums (referred to as "mansions"). At the same time, the pursuit by some firms of easy profits led to a decline in standards. Overall, the housing industry was brought about by the government's poorly thought-out housing

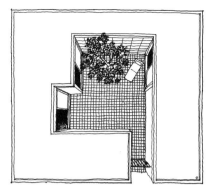

Court

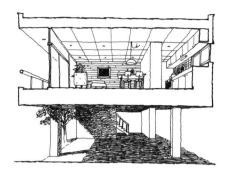

Piloti

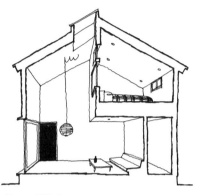

Open Well

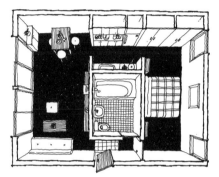

Core System

policy, which failed to meet the needs of ordinary people.

Thus, while the housing industry and professional architects have continued in many ways to improve the state of housing in modern Japan, the individual attempting to build a new home still faces many obstacles, including inevitable legal restrictions. The biggest obstacle, in light of overcrowded conditions throughout the country, is the practical question of how to make optimal use of what is inevitably a small lot of land to build upon.

Ingenious efforts of all kinds have been made to design attractive homes within confined spaces, many of which have proved applicable to apartment houses as well. These include the use of courtyards, piloti, open wells, and core systems (see illustrations above).

Houses or apartments with courtyards are eminently suitable to city life in that they incorporate light, air, and an outside view while maintaining the privacy of the inhabitants. Houses or offices raised on piloti or stilts make advantageous use of limited lots by creating an open space beneath the structure that can be put to various uses. Houses with open wells spanning several floors can create a sense of unconfined space that would otherwise be difficult in a small structure; skylights at the top of the well can also introduce light and promote the aura of expansiveness. Structures employing a core system—whether homes or office buildings— concentrate certain facilities in one area for economical construction or for protection against earthquake and fire.

Housing in Japan Today

Housing conditions in Japan today are largely the result of changes that have taken place since the Meiji Restoration and, more particularly, since the end of World War II, as we have already seen. The most prominent trend over this period is most certainly the development of apartment buildings of more than six stories and complexes of high-rise multi-unit dwellings (*danchi*; see p. 112). This fact does not deny the significance of suburban housing developments; nor does it turn a blind eye to the continued construction of more traditional homes in agricultural communities. Even in large metropolitan areas, many people live in inherited family homes or in newly built houses. In fact, a majority of Japanese still live in detached houses, not in apartments or high-rises. Nevertheless, it remains a fact that the development, and transformation over time, of multi-unit high-rise dwellings is a hallmark feature of the modern urban scene, where the greater part of the population will continue to make its living.

In 1955, as mentioned earlier (pp. 114-115), the Japan Housing Corporation (Nihon Jūtaku Kōdan) was established, and the high-rise multi-unit dwellings that it promoted began to appear in the latter half of the fifties. Sleeping and eating areas had until then occupied the same area; the aim now was to make them separate. The result was an apartment unit commonly called a 2DK (two rooms with a dining-kitchen area).

The advent of the 2DK was a defining event, but when the economy entered a high-growth phase in the 1960s, and televisions and other electric appliances started to flood the market, the 2DK was no longer seen as sufficiently spacious and began to undergo transformation. Among the more affluent, the need for increased space was met by larger and more expensive condominiums called "mansions." As the economy was further stimulated by such events as the 1964 Tokyo Olympics and the opening of "bullet train" service between Osaka

and Tokyo, the "mansion" eventually began to replace the more confined, ordinary apartment.

In 1972 the prime minister of the day, Kakuei Tanaka, proposed a "remodeling" of the country: that is, a geographical redistribution of industry away from the Tokyo-Osaka belt to regional centers linked by superhighways and bullet trains. This led to a period of intense activity in construction, communications, and housing. Housing was further spurred by the coming of age of the baby-boomer generation and the proliferation of the nuclear family. As a result, high-rise multi-unit dwellings and "new town" complexes (see p. 113) became increasingly common. The number of apartment units in high-rise buildings stood at 50,000 in 1968 and 325,000 in 1973, and these figures contin-

ued to grow thereafter to 1,410,000 in 1983, 2,071,000 in 1988, and 2,921,000 in 1993.

In the early 1980s, the economy entered into a phase characterized by easy credit, unrestrained speculation, and high prices, commonly referred to as the "bubble economy." Houses on lots and "mansions" were seen as areas of prime investment, and many different types of dwellings at various prices were produced. After the bursting of the bubble in 1989–90, prices went down, investment fell off, and homes and "mansions" came to be built that were more suited to the real needs of the occupants.

The types of "mansions" produced at this time can be categorized into urban, suburban, and resort types, or alternatively into permanent family types, one-room types for those tem-

porarily stationed away from home, and homes for the elderly.

One recent trend is the "two-generation" mansion for extended families, which arose from concern over the upbringing of children in homes where both parents worked and from the need to keep the cost of housing grandparents, parents, and children within reasonable bounds. The Housing Loan Corporation has given support to this type of dwelling since 1980. The "two-generation" mansion shows a number of innovations, with separate toilets and kitchens for the two households but a common living room in which all members can gather. It is to be hoped that innovation of this type will continue in all areas of housing in the years to come.

INDEX

Kotohira 88
kudo type 73
kudzu 11
Kumamoto prefecture 73
kumi-gashira 61
kuni ("state") 11, 22
Kyoto 44, 48-52, 56, 59-60, 70, 74, 77-78, 90-91
Kyūshū 18, 29, 101

L
L-shaped floor plan (*magari-ya*) 66
Lake Biwa 70
lamp stands 31
land tenants (*jigari*) 74
landlords 45, 48, 56, 62, 79
landowners (*jinushi*) 74, 100
Left Capital 32, 48
long-handled planes (*yariganna*) 26, 58
low-cost housing 110

M
machi (district) 74
machi-bugyō (magistrate) 74
machi-hikeshi (firefighters) 74, 77
machi-kaisho 74
machiya 28, 33
maebiki-noko 58
magari-ya ("bent house") 66, 67
magistrate (*machi-bugyō*) 74
manors 45
"mansions" 112, 114, 116, 117
Man'yōshū 28
markets 32, 48, 51, 88
marriage 40, 53
master carpenters (*tōryō*) 90; see also *carpenters*
mat makers 74
mats 31, 34, 40, 45, 50, 55, 64-65, 70; see also *tatami*
Matsumoto-daira 69
Medieval period 43-46, 50, 53, 60, 62, 74, 82, 90
Meiji government 94, 100
Meiji period 93-94, 101-102, 105-106, 108
Meiji Restoration 93-94, 116
Meiji, Emperor 93
merchants 28, 32-33, 48, 51, 59-60, 74-75, 77-79, 83, 85, 89, 96
metal fittings 42
Miike mine 101
Minami-Kawachi 71
Minamoto Yoritomo 43
minato-machi (harbor towns) 88
mines and miners 94, 100-101
minimal housing 110
Ministry of Industrial Works (Kōbushō) 94

miscanthus grass 91
misedana ("display shelves") 48, 50
miso 61
miyako 32
moated tomb 19
modernization 93, 100-101, 107
modules 57-58
Momoyama period 43, 58
money economy 51, 89
monzen-machi (temple town) 88
movable partitions 111
movable stove 50
moya 33-34, 36, 40, 52
Muku-ryō 56
mura (village) 18; see also *village*
Murakami family 68
Murata Jukō 85
Muromachi period 43, 44, 47, 52, 54
mushiko-mado 78

N
Nabe-machi 74
Nagano prefecture 65, 69
Nagaoka 38
Nagasaki 89, 94
Nagata-chō 95
nagaya (rowhouses) 45, 75, 79, 81, 87, 101, 105-106
nagaya-mon (rowhouse gates) 61, 71, 87
nakama (guild) 90; see also *guilds*
nakanoma 65
Naka-Sendō 88
Nakatsumichi 35
Nanbu district 66
nando 47, 62, 64, 70
nando-gamae 55
Naniwa capital 35
Nara 30, 48, 51-52, 56, 71, 88
Nara basin 22
Nara period 28-29, 36, 42, 44
Nara prefecture 22
narabi-kura (paired storehouses) 71
Narita 88
Natsume Sōseki 94
natural features 10
naya (shed) 78
"new towns," 112, 113, 116
Niigata prefecture 65, 67
nijiriguchi 85
Nintoku 22
Nishiyama 70
niuji 70
Nō 82, 85
nokogiri 58